SECRETS OF GETTING YOUR BOOK PUBLISHED

To Rob, for being my rock. Without your unending patience, support and encouragement, my becoming an author would not be a reality.

SECRETS OF GETTING YOUR BOOK PUBLISHED

Elise Vachon

UNION SQUARE PUBLISHING

First Edition
First Printing   *August 2003*

Copyright © 2003 by Elise Vachon
-All Rights Reserved-

All brand names and product names used in this book are trademarks, registered trademarks, or trade names of their respective holders.

Library of Congress Catalogue Card Number: 2003100440
ISBN: 1-58042-112-1

UNION SQUARE PUBLISHING
An Imprint of Cardoza Publishing
P.O. Box 1500, Cooper Station, New York, NY 10276
Phone 1-800-577-WINS
www.cardozapub.com

TABLE OF CONTENTS

5. COMPETITION 73

6. PROMOTION & MARKETING 89

7. THE FINAL TWO PARTS 107

8. SAGE ADVICE   121

9. WHAT YOU NEED & WANT   135

1. AT THE STARTING LINE

What to Expect

The prospect of writing a book is intimidating. The problem, as I see it, is that most people are afraid of the complicated process and never take that first step. My goal is to remove the anxiety and lead you through that process step by step.

Rest assured — it requires hard work, commitment and a great deal of discipline. But at the end of it all, I have confidence you can be the proud parent of a published book distributed at book outlets across the country!

If you are a writer by trade, things may be a little easier as you are formally trained in the art of stringing together words, sentences, paragraphs and chapters. However, if you aren't an author you can still learn to produce a credible proposal and eventually bring forth a book.

Besides hard work and discipline, you'll need a great deal of patience. Going from A to Z in the publishing world takes time. First you have to write the proposal, then distribute it. When someone eventually buys the proposal, you negotiate the contract and finally agree to a timeline for manuscript delivery.

From the moment you conceive a book idea to the time it actually comes out in print and sits on the bookstore shelf can be one to two years.

As an author, you can expect that your friends, family and those you meet will be very impressed with the fact that you have a book published. The reality, however, is that there is little glamour or fame in book writing or publishing unless you are a famous person already.

Another sad fact is that most authors' books don't generate

a big fat check. In fact, if you get published at all, you'll probably make a very modest advance (somewhere between $1,000 and $10,000) if you're lucky and nothing more.

So why do writers write books? Because they love it and it's in their blood to do so. We are artists and love what we do. Creative people must create or wither. We hope that one day we can make a great living by doing what we are passionate about, but in the mean time we are content striving to achieve that goal.

Unfortunately, you can expect that, no matter how marvelous a writer you are, your proposal will be rejected many times. Of course, being a good writer is important, if not critical, but being able to put together a stellar proposal and marketing plan is even more important. It doesn't matter how great the writing is if your initial presentation stinks.

This book mainly addresses the traditional form of publishing, in which an author prepares a book proposal, that author is contracted by the publisher to write the book, and the publisher agrees to incur all costs associated with producing, marketing, distributing and selling the book.

We will also cover important details such as advances and/or royalties from the publisher and the author's obligations to write and deliver the book meeting all agreed upon specifications. I've included some reference to self-publishing and Internet publishing as these can tie in with conventional publishing.

This book will guide you through the different stages of putting together a book proposal, presenting it and writing your manuscript. Most of the instruction deals with to non-fiction and how-to books, but you'll also have enough information at the end of it all to get around in the publishing maze. You will be able to submit fiction, non-fiction and children's (fiction and non-fiction) book proposals to any publisher by following the basic steps.

Don't expect the first publisher you contact to publish your book. When you feel like you're getting to the end of your rope, don't give up. Remember, editors and publishers are simply people. They are in this business to make money, have a little fun and give the world a good book selection.

Expect to get treated as you would in any other venue in life: sometimes well, sometimes shabbily. Use humor to keep it light and use a pleasant conversational tone. It lets the editors know they are working with an interesting human being and someone who might be fun to get to know.

The more considerate you are, the more you'll be appreciated by the editors and publishers. Perhaps you can expect a little kinder treatment if you are as thoughtful and professional as you can possibly be.

Deciding What to Write

The *Association of American University Presses Directory* (AAUP Directory) may be just the place to look if you want to write an academic book. This directory lists all the university presses and their relevant contact information.

Most of the titles produced by university presses are dry textbooks or academic in nature. This may suit you and your writing goals. However, if you don't want to write academic books and you can't decide what to write, the AAUP is still a possibility for finding university presses that want to publish less scholarly books with the idea of making a larger profit.

Call and speak to someone in the sales department and ask for most recent trade catalog. You may have to beg a little to get one because the directories aren't usually given out for free.

In the catalog, you may find, for example, that they are searching for someone to write a book on the migratory patterns of the Monarch butterfly. If you think this is something you could do well, call to make sure they don't have the title in the works, and then put together your proposal.

To find the "flavor" of books a certain publisher goes for, try their catalogs. It's a little more time consuming way of coming up with ideas for a book, but it might work for you. It's not a common practice among writers to do so, but it sometimes gives insight into how particular publishers work.

If the publishing house is a small one, you may ask for the sales department and end up speaking to one person who wears many or all hats. Don't get caught unprepared or get rattled if this is the case.

I believe most people have an interesting story to tell, whether it's fiction or non-fiction. The adage "Write what you know" still holds true. If you are an expert gardener, fisherman, tile cutter, seamstress, historical re-enactor, financial whiz, mechanic or story teller, you have at least one book in you. If you can teach someone how to do something or have a lively imagination, you can write a book. Take it step-by-step and slowly it will come to be.

For example, I have a friend who is a personal fitness trainer. He firmly believes his methods and techniques are better than those of other instructors he observes in his daily work-life at the gym. He is determined to share his formula for fitness training in a book, and we are currently fine-tuning his proposal.

In my case, I'm from Kenya. I've lived all over the world. I have a passion for travel and spent a lot of time in Belize. So once I decided to write a book (it took quite a few years for me to get serious!), It seemed natural that it should be a travel book on Belize.

Many months later and after a great deal of research, I finally felt I understood how the book publishing process worked and I was ready to get to work. About two years later my book on Kenya, yes Kenya, was published. The publisher liked my proposal on Belize but already had a book about that country, so he asked me to write a book on Kenya instead. My efforts still paid off, but not quite as I thought they would.

I have the advantage of being a magazine editor by trade, but despite this, I felt anxious about the unknowns of the book industry. I noticed there wasn't much written guidance available, so I kept the idea of a book on publishing and proposal writing in the back of my mind.

Once people knew I had a book published and often asked me "How did you do it?" I began to share with these friends and acquaintances the "how-tos" of book proposal writing. One thing led to another, and, once my Kenya book was in its second edition, I was ready to tackle a proposal for this book.

Now let me qualify what I just told you. In order to write a book, I don't necessarily believe you have to be an expert on your subject. Clearly, it's easier to write on a subject if you are proficient at it. But, if you want to write non-fiction books for a living you can't possibly be an expert on everything.

After you write your book, it's likely you'll be an authority

— that's one of the great things about being a writer, you get to learn all kinds of new stuff as you go along, and you get to meet some great people (and possibly animals) too.

You do, however, have to put a convincing book proposal together if you want a publisher to buy it. You must be able to demonstrate clearly your knowledge on the subject in your table of contents and outline.

Publishers expect the chapter outline to be concise and intelligent. Don't try to throw something together you if haven't researched the basics. You must be convincing, and you must show that you can write about the subject well.

Even in fiction writing you are often required to do extensive research on a particular subject. For example, if your main character is a ballistics expert, but you know nothing about guns, you'll need to find people who are knowledgeable, pick their brains and research the subject so you can write accurately and expertly.

When you're trying to decide what to write, run your idea by a few people and see what kind of reaction they have. Ask your spouse, parents, friends, the librarian and your neighbors. Ask them to be honest — you don't want to waste your time if everyone thinks your idea won't fly. Pay close attention to their body language — this can be key when they don't want to hurt your feelings.

Some writers won't discuss their ideas with anyone. That's okay, too. Many believe that if you talk about the idea too much or for too long, the energy, momentum and follow-through are lost. Instead of writing, you are talking. You'll eventually figure out what works for you.

One key factor in deciding what to write is passion. You can't write about something in which you have no feeling for or interest. So find your passions and you'll find your subjects.

Self Confidence Factor

It's critical to make up your mind firmly that you're going to achieve your goal of writing a great book proposal, selling it to a publisher and finishing the manuscript on time. Without determination and belief in your abilities, it simply won't happen. I know so many people who dream about writing the "great American novel" or who have even written a few chapters, but who never got it done because they lacked the determination. Don't let yourself become one of those folks.

The odds seem overwhelmingly against your ever being published, but it's a certainty you won't be published if you don't try. Without effort, there is no reward.

Many of the publishing houses, particularly the very large ones, don't accept any unsolicited proposals. This is because they have the cream of the writing crop to choose from and don't feel the need to take a chance on a new writer. However, there are many more that will.

Those publishers who do accept unsolicited proposals and manuscripts may receive thousands a day! Knowing that, you should find it easy to understand reluctance on the part of a publishing house to work with unfamiliar and unsolicited authors. It also makes it critical that your proposal be as perfect in every detail as you can make it. When you do this, your odds increase significantly. It also takes faith on your part that the work is good enough to submit. I am certain you can do it.

I heard one editor at a writer's conference say that she doesn't mind too much if an author calls her to suggest and idea. It's refreshing to find editors that are willing to show compassion to a novice. I'll grant you that it is rare, but you might just be fortunate enough to find the one.

If you do get through to an editor on the phone, keep your call short and to the point. Be confident and self-assured but not cocky. Tell the editor you are writing a book proposal on whatever the subject is, and see if it's a title which interests him or her. Or call and ask what kind of titles the publisher is seeking. Then you can write your proposal to fit his or her needs. If the editor seeks a writer for some obscure book idea that no one could ever possibly guess, you might just be in luck.

The bottom line is, no matter what you want or choose to write, you must, above all else, have self-confidence and perseverance. Your success is entirely dependent on your trust in yourself and the adherence to the course of action you select. Without these traits, I guarantee you won't get your books published.

What Book Publishers Want

Publishers are often over worked and underpaid like the rest of us. Try to keep this in mind when writing your proposal. Give them the answers to the key questions they'll ask when reviewing your book proposal, and you'll raise the probability of getting published.

Be sure to include answers to the following questions:

1. Why am I uniquely qualified to write this proposal?

2. Is this book worth $19.95 (or whatever price you suggest) and will people buy it?

3. What is better or singular about my book compared to others out there?

4. Is what I have to say enough to fill a book?

5. Are there enough readers/aficionados in the world to justify producing this book?

If your answers are enough to satisfy you, then chances are they will persuade a publisher and you may get an opportunity to have your book published.

Think of things from the publisher's perspective. He or she has to like your idea enough to contract you to write it, pay you an advance, and arrange to have the book printed, distributed and sold. That's quite a commitment. It shows a great deal of confidence in an author's abilities to write and come through on time. They need you to deliver.

Once your idea passes the various levels of consent and makes the final cut within the house, it's time for the publisher to present the proposal to the editorial board. They meet every couple of months to discuss all potential book ideas and to extend the go-ahead if those ideas meet the prescribed criteria. It's common for a publishing house to have a board of directors or an editorial board responsible for giving final approval on any book deals. The publisher counts on your proposal to sell itself to every level of authority it passes through.

Publishers are in business to make money. Each time they take on an inexperienced writer, they are making a huge gamble and hoping the author can actually do what he says he can. Now, perhaps, you can understand why it's so difficult to get a publisher to invest in an idea from a new writer.

When the publishing house staff receives a proposal, they expect it to be first-class and they expect to be sold on a book concept. It's up to you to show what you can do. A strong proposal is your foot in the door.

Most of the big publishing houses are in New York. If you plan on targeting these companies take a moment to ask yourself if the potential audience is large enough to warrant their investing in your book. They are definitely not interested in anything that is written for a small, specialized readership. If, for example, you are writing a book for supermarket deli managers in Georgia (*How to Manage your Deli Counter More Effectively and Increase Sales*) and you can show that there are only 45,000 potential buyers, the book won't fly.

The standard formula for the average book's sales says that of the total number of people who might be interested in the book's subject matter, only one to two percent actually buy it. This is what any major publisher anticipates when committing to a new book.

The first run of a book is usually a minimum number of copies, and the publisher expects to sell them all. If they don't all sell, then chances are that the publisher made a poor investment. Your deli managers' book will sell only about 885 copies — certainly not enough to pique the interest of a major publishing player, and, really not enough to make your work effort worthwhile.

What big publishing companies look for are book ideas that grab the attention of a very large part of the general population. When their books go onto bookstore shelves, they want the titles to jump out and appeal to most of the people who walk through the door. There are many, many potential audiences a publisher would be interested in, for example: business owners, outdoor enthusiasts, parents, teenagers, seniors, car devotees, computer owners, gardeners and pet enthusiasts, just to mention a few.

The worst thing you can do to yourself is submit inadequate information to the publisher to-be. At the very least, the publisher expects to see an outline, a table of contents, and the specifications to your book. If you present a great proposal with all the parts I suggest, chances are, someone will recognize the effort you put into it. He or she might even send you a one-line critique.

It stands to reason that a good proposal shows you are a thorough writer and can generate a good manuscript.

A friend of mine, before we knew each other, wrote a (fiction) book. Now he wants to get it published. As he already put all the work into writing it, I suggested he send in two complete chapters along with all the other sections I recommended. What he wanted to do was send in bits and pieces of four or five chapters. I explained this isn't what a publisher wants to see. It would be a mistake. All he'd accomplish would be totally confusing and frustrating the receiving editor. The snippets wouldn't give the publisher a clear picture of the book. Instead, there would be a sense of chaos with no clear indication of the style or content.

A publisher/editor acquaintance says her hair stands on end when she opens a package and sees a ream of disheveled papers with no page numbers or cover letter. Immediately she has a bad impression of the writer and would rather not try to figure out the mess and wade through the proposal. Almost inevitably, the writer ends up with a rejection letter.

This same editor shares that she gets angry knots in her stomach when she opens a submission envelope only to find a short letter saying, "I have an idea for a book on tomatoes. Do you want to buy it?" Obviously, she never does.

Publishing isn't for the frail or for those unwilling to tackle a sometimes overwhelming task. But I hope this book gives you the insight into understanding what publishers expect, what makes a proposal good, how to submit it, how to ask the right questions and how the system works.

What I'm saying is, if you're serious about writing a book and getting it published, give the publishers what they want. Go the extra mile to prepare a perfect book proposal. If you aren't willing to do this, then go back to watching television.

The Cover Letter

The cover letter is the first thing a potential editor or publisher sees. It's imperative you pay close attention to this correspondence by making it professional and, at the same time, attention-grabbing.

The cover letter should be no longer than one page and must

quickly convey what is enclosed in the envelope. Try to keep this letter down to two or three paragraphs. All you really want to achieve here is to get the editor to look at the rest of the pages in your proposal.

Naturally, you must include your name, address and contact information. The opening line should say what you have sent them and why. Take the opportunity to make a strong sales pitch. If you're writing a cookbook for family pets use a hook something like this: "Sixty-two percent of American homes have a furry resident. There are 40 million households with dogs and 37.4 million homes with cats. Many of them are on a 'natural' treat frenzy. The hottest trend in the pet world today revolves around buying and baking wholesome treats for our canine and feline friends."

Now tell them you propose to write a "natural" book for those people and their pets. Then introduce yourself and your credentials. End by thanking them for their time and for looking at the enclosed proposal. Include a self-addresses stamped envelope (SASE).

Humor is good. A quick wit and sense of humor in your cover letter shows you'll be fun to work with. In addition, being funny gives a sense of who you are — on an even keel and confident enough not to take yourself too seriously.

Sometimes, of course, the material you propose may not lend itself to humor. In that case, stay away from it. You certainly don't want to offend the people you are trying to impress. But in general, I'd say most topics have a humorous side that can be touched on in an attention-grabbing letter.

I don't know anyone who doesn't like to laugh. Once you get someone laughing he automatically likes you a little better. If you make an editor laugh, in all likelihood, he won't put your proposal down (even if it's just to see what else there is to laugh at).

Query Letter

The query letter is a quicker (but not necessarily better) way of selling a book to a publisher without the details found in a proposal.

The sole purpose of the query (or inquiry) letter is to tell the editors quickly and succinctly what you want to write about and to see if they are interested in pursuing the possibility of publishing a book on the subject.

A great query letter concisely tells an editor the who, what, where, when and how of your idea. Consider it a letter of introduction to you, your writing abilities and your book idea without the attachment of the complete proposal.

Keep your letter to one page or two if you absolutely have to. Keep it simple and to the point. Use professional looking letterhead if you have it or at least quality paper. Get the name of the editor right and double check the spelling. Be enthusiastic. Tell your reader that you want to get your idea published as a book. Don't go into great detail and be formal without being stuffy.

Creatively describe (don't tell but show) what your book is about and who the potential buyers are. Explain why you think the editor you are writing to will be interested in your work and give that editor a possible delivery date and manuscript length.

Include suggestions on what sources you can use, who you might interview and what reference books are available. If you have some unlikely and interesting statistics or anecdotes on your topic, use them.

Include a little about yourself and your credentials but keep this to a bare minimum. Finally, give your phone number and e-mail address in case an editor wants to reach you. End by thanking them for their time and asking if they would like to know or see more. Include a SASE.

Some writers would rather send out a query letter than a book proposal, as it's easier and faster. This is an acceptable course of action although I prefer the book proposal method because I feel it's much more thorough.

When you get to the point of looking for potential editors and publishing houses, you may notice they actually stipulate which they prefer — a query letter or proposal. In many instances the publisher wants a query letter first, and if they like what they see, they'll ask for a full-blown proposal.

A query letter gives you the opportunity to focus your thoughts and streamline what you have in mind. However, in my opinion, the letter, no matter how carefully written, doesn't give the editor the full picture of your capabilities.

Naturally, it takes a lot more research time to prepare a proposal than it does to write a letter, but in my experience they sell more books.

A successful fellow writer who prefers to use a query letter over a proposal made a good point in favor of the letter. He says a good query letter helps the writer convey the substance of the book and avoids rejections based on style. This is a valid argument, as at this stage in the sale of a book idea you want them to buy the concept not the style.

However, if the style you're worried about is your writing voice you may win the battle but lose the war when they discover and dislike your technique or approach later on.

I find that editors (and agents if you're seeking one) quickly and with little guilt say thanks but no thanks to a letter. After all, they ask themselves, "How much effort and time went into producing this letter?" Not much, right? We know that's not entirely true either, but honestly, the letter is quicker to write than the proposal.

On the other hand, a 30-page book proposal with careful research included means more to that same editor. It'll be obvious that you are serious and took great pains to do the work. She will feel obligated to take a closer look if she's any kind of human being at all despite how overworked she is. I believe the additional effort pays off. It did for me.

I knew exactly what kind of book I wanted to write. I was very focused and knew that only that type of book would do, so I was resolved to go the extra mile in preparing the proposal. I knew it was one essential step in the journey to get my book into print. If I hadn't been so determined to stick with my subject matter, I might have considered query letters instead. With the query letter it would be less time consuming to put an idea together. I could send out more ideas to more publishers within a shorter timeframe.

It stands to reason that basic etiquette applies to all letters including query letters. For example, you certainly won't have a prayer if you insult the editor by telling her you hate the publishing industry, or you don't think editors are honest. By the same token, don't put yourself down by saying you are a poor writer, you don't know if you have the time but you'll try if they pay you very well or anything else to that effect. I really shouldn't even have to say these things as common sense should prevail, but you never know.

Let me add a word of caution: most editors and publishers resent getting phone calls instead of query letters or book proposals. (I know because I was one of those editors.) If you decide to pursue a publisher this way, expect to get a rather cold reception most of the time.

Editors are busy people, and unless they are particularly easy going and magnanimous, they will quickly say no and shut you down, if you manage to get through to them in the first place. Unless you are spectacularly talented in making this type of phone call, choose the letter or proposal route.

The same goes for the e-mail query. E-mail is quick, easy and effortless to send. It's also without great exertion that editors delete it. Therefore, it's my recommendation not to use e-mail as your method for idea delivery unless you know the editor or have been asked to do so.

Should you choose to go the e-mail route, at least be certain your correspondence is perfect both in terms of content and spelling. Also be careful to whom you address it and how many people you send it to. The rules of multiple submission elsewhere in this book apply.

Taking the query letter route, if that's what you decide, should involve some careful writing and probably several re-writings. In other words, the letter should be perfect. According to all the writers I know (myself included), a great query letter takes at least three re-writes if not more to be exquisite. This letter, after all, is going to make the publisher or editor pay you millions for the manuscript!

If the query letter is directed at an agent because you want him or her to take you on as a client, the same rules and suggestions apply. They must weed through piles of correspondence to find a new writer and are generally (just like publishers) looking for innovative ideas and expertly drafted letters.

After one month of waiting patiently, feel free to send a polite follow-up letter, e-mail or phone call to see what the status of your inquiry is. But don't waste time being pushy. If you don't get a response, assume the answer is no and move on.

There's no right or wrong answer here. After considering all the facts and options, only you can decide on what route to take; query letter or comprehensive proposal. Remember however, that the greater the effort, the greater the return.

The Title Page

Keep this page simple, clean and uncomplicated. It's the second page a book publisher sees after your cover letter. Here's where you can make a significant impression by paying attention to the details. If this page is ugly, cluttered or dirty, you may have lost the edge over other proposals.

Chose a simple typeface, something you use all the time. My preference is Times New Roman, which is a standard. It's acceptable to use 12 point type for all the text but go up in size on the title to perhaps 14 or 16 point type, and make it bold.

The text placement can vary, but I'd recommend centering it in the middle of the page. My method is to put the book title on the first line; the words Book Proposal on the second line, my name, address phone number, fax number, web site and e-mail address on the subsequent lines.

If you have an agent and you want the publisher to deal with him or her directly, then include his or her contact information and make note of the fact you want your agent to be contacted. If you have an agent, it would seem a little strange that you would be making the contact. After all isn't this your agent's job? But, publishing procedures aren't carved in stone; they vary widely). You may want to consider leaving your contact information off altogether, but it if the publisher has a question the agent can't answer it might be handy for him or her to have it.

Definite Don'ts

If you have already written your book and now want to learn the secrets of submitting it to a publisher, resist the temptation to send in the entire manuscript. Whatever you do, please don't mail in a huge box with 2,000 pieces of paper enclosed. Instead, take the time to prepare the proposal as I'm suggesting.

Editors hate getting a package with reams of paper in it weighing more than their dogs. No one at the publishing house has time to read the tome, and handling it, along with the other hundreds of proposals sitting around, is simply an unreasonable expectation. Besides, it shows you don't know how the process works.

Don't rely on spell checker. Think for yourself — definitely don't let the computer do it for you. Often, in books on publishing, you'll encounter a little poem that'll make you smile whenever you think of the spell-check option on your computer. I think it speaks clearly as to the shortcomings of spell-check and the pitfalls of letting it dictate which words to use and what grammar is appropriate:

I have a spelling checker,
It came with my PC;
It plainly marks for my revue
Mistakes I cannot see.
I've run this poem threw it,
I'm sure your please to no,
Its letter perfect in it's weigh,
My checker tolled me sew.

Checklist: Critical Parts of a Book Proposal

In order to produce the best possible book proposal you can, it's essential that you include all the sections I'm about to mention. It's also important that each of these sections begins on a new page. Use this list as a book proposal checklist and arrange your documents in this order.

1. Cover Letter

A short letter to state who you are, catch the publisher's attention regarding your book's subject, and ask him or her to take a look at your book idea.

2. Title Page

This should be the very first page the publisher sees after your cover letter. It includes the title and all contact information.

3. Summary

Here you explain the book's subject, why it's captivating to your potential readers, and why the public needs this book.

4. Specifications

This section describes the number of chapters you're planning, how many pages, how you will organize and format, paperback or hardcover, the size, and how many and what kind of graphics/illustrations you are including.

5. Market

When you're putting together this section, use statistics to emphasize the size of the market. Explain how many of these people there are and why they would want to buy this book.

6. Promotion

Present any ideas that can be adopted by the publisher to promote and sell your book.

7. Competition

Research and compile a list of any books that compete with yours.

8. Author's Bio

Write a short and simple resume describing why you are the prefect person to write this book.

9. Outline

Describe, chapter by chapter, the detailed contents of your book. Use a plain and simple framework.

2. THE SUMMARY

A Detailed Look at the Selling Summary

This is probably the most important part of your proposal. Here, you summarize what the book is about, explain why anyone would want to buy it, detail whom you'll write it for and why it's better and different than any other books available.

The summary is just that — a brief and succinct sketch of your book idea. Later in your proposal, when you put together the table of contents and outline, you get into more detail of what's in the manuscript.

To begin this summary section, write two or three paragraphs encapsulating what the book is about. This copy should intrigue and hold the interest of your editor compelling her to read on.

Once you've got their attention, you can keep that grip by going into two or three paragraphs of why someone would buy your book and read it. How it helps them (if it's non-fiction) or how it entertains them (if it's fiction). It's critical for you to describe why readers want to buy your book and why they will think it is important to their lives because this is the publisher's clue as to how many books will sell.

Next, you need to briefly fill in the blanks as to why your book will be superior and distinct when compared to others. The summary (and the entire proposal for that matter) is interwoven and inextricably tied together. Much of the information you use here, is also be part of the "Competition" and "Market" sections later on in your proposal.

Getting the facts across to the editor or publisher must be swift. I'd suggest packing a punch in the first two paragraphs of your summary. If you don't catch their attention quickly, they

25

may move on to the next book proposal in the stack.

Why is Your Book Better?

When I prepared the proposal for this book, I said, "*Getting Your Book Published* is a paperback book for anyone who writes a book or has a good book idea and wants to get that book published (this may include the entire adult world!) It will be a short, easy to read, step-by-step, meat-and-potatoes book filled with content and not frills. It will be invaluable to both the serious book writer and the beginning writer who thinks he/she can write a publishable book. It will make their life as an author easier and will teach them how to sell their book to a publisher."

I explained that this book would be superior and easier to read than others on the market because I would organize the material in a more logical fashion — a systematic progression of the necessary steps. I said the book would contain only the key information to get a book sold/published, making it very easy to use.

In addition, I used my personal experiences and research while trying to get my first book sold, saying there simply wasn't much available to guide me through the steps of how to get published. There was plenty on how to write a book, but not enough on the details of how to get a publishing house to buy the book.

Making the point that your book is both better and different will, we hope, snare the publisher. The more innovative your angle, the better. Of course, you don't want to come up with an angle that's so bizarre no one would ever think of it much less want to buy the book. Or maybe that's your intention and for the right publisher this might just work.

The most commonly used hooks in a summary explain that your book has better organization of the chapters or material, includes topics not covered in other books, or offers a unique slant toward a different audience or group.

If other books have drawings and graphics, say that yours won't and explain why this is better for the reader. Say, for example, that the drawings are distracting because they don't help or show any useful information. Show that without graphics your book will be more compact and easier to carry around.

When "shopping" around, if you find comparable books are

short and to the point, say yours will be much longer and more detailed and why this might hook more readers. Look inside the competition and try to pinpoint what they left out, then say you will cover those things in your book to make it more informative.

If your book is primarily for entertainment, then drop in the most fascinating details and highlights you have, like a movie preview. The tidbits serve as a hook. Now you simply reel in the publishing house. What you want to achieve in the summary is for the editor to say she would love to read the rest of the story.

If your book will help the reader stay young, be more graceful, more interesting, be richer, wiser, happier, healthier or accomplish any other positive quality say so in your proposal and say so often.

People who buy books want to either be entertained or learn something and publishers know this. It's their business to know. Now you know it too and can give them what they, and ultimately their readers, want.

Can You Write?

An editor working for a trade publisher once said that people who could not write wrote ninety-eight percent of the materials she received from unsolicited authors. That's rather a frightening statement. She also said that most of the time she based her decision on whether to consider the manuscript or not on how well it was written. That's a tough stance, but when you think about it, it makes sense. A publisher's buying a poorly written book would be like a furniture distributor's selling furnishings made by someone who wasn't a carpenter.

When dealing with an unpublished author, most editors or publishers want to make sure you can write. It stands to reason that even if you have a good idea for a book but you aren't a writer by profession, there may be doubts regarding your ability.

So how can you show your potential buyer that you will come through with a well-written manuscript?

The answer, of course, is to present your book proposal in the most professional manner possible. Make sure your pages are crisp and clean. Organize the sections inside carefully and clearly. Check your spelling and grammar often. Write, re-write and have another person who is qualified edit the proposal.

Getting around the writing problem, if you have one, may not be too difficult. You could go back to school and take English grammar and writing classes. Work with your professor/teacher on the ins and outs of writing until you and he feel you're ready to take on the task of writing a book. You might even consider using your book as your class project. That way the teacher is there to guide you through the writing, editing, and learning process.

Find a writing partner — someone who is compatible with you and can share many hours of dedicated writing-time. An added advantage to teaming up with another writer is that you can help pull each other out of a slump or writer's block. It's much easier to get and give encouragement as a team.

This partner should, of course, be a writer who understands what your book proposal and book are about and can put these together in the way you envision. He should be someone who can write and share ideas without getting on your nerves. If you go this route, agree — in writing — before you begin, how to fairly share the work, the accolades and the royalties.

Many writers share books as co-authors, there's no shame in that. In fact, it's probably easier to divide the load and the research with another person. The problem might be in deciding who gets first billing.

It's not uncommon for an aspiring book author to use a ghostwriter. A ghostwriter crafts the actual text as you dictate the ideas and thoughts. Many celebrities use ghostwriters in order to get their stories into print. Sometimes the contract states the author's name won't be seen or mentioned and sometimes the credit is shared. Hiring a ghostwriter, of course, costs money, but this might be worked out as a percentage of the royalties.

If you can't write well but really want to get published, my final suggestion is to hire an editor to edit your final draft for you. I know several editors who, for a reasonable price, can put your book or proposal into the shape it should be in for submission. The fee depends on the hours of work involved.

The Slant

Whether you choose to go with a query letter or a full-blown proposal the secret to selling your work is the angle or slant you present to a prospective book publisher.

Most of us know the subjects covered in most books have been done and done again. We see this when we go to the library or the bookstore and browse the titles on the shelves. This is particularly true of non-fiction and perhaps not quite so obviously true in fiction.

If you're really good, you'll be able to find a subject or topic that has never covered before. But finding a never-before-covered book idea is a tough proposition so you may have to apply those brain cells and come up with a new angle or slant on an old subject.

You may not have any books to your credit, but a unique slant makes an editor sit up and take notice — and perhaps even ask for more details on the book.

As I mentioned before, when working on ideas for saleable books you want to keep in mind that readers want to be entertained with fiction or bettered in some way with non-fiction. They want to learn something, be taught how to do something or improve their life someway. Find the slant that no one else has thought of and you'll have a winner.

Agents and Author's Representatives

As I mentioned previously, publishing houses, particularly the large ones, very often won't accept unsolicited manuscripts of any kind. If someone called to ask about a submission he or she would likely be told that, without an agent, there's no getting an editor to take a look at your proposal. Some are a little more lenient and accept book proposals from authors who have at least one published book.

The logic behind a publisher not accepting proposals from anyone other than agents is simply to help weed out the less desirable submissions. An agent becomes a screen. If the proposal makes it past the agent, it's more likely to be something a publisher is interested in.

When an agent is willing to put his or her reputation on the line, the publisher or editor takes that as a good sign. Agents spend their working lives looking at proposals and discussing book ideas with their stable of writers. They act as a sounding board for ideas that may be of interest to an author, but in reality are simply not good book topics.

Typically, out of the thousands of publishing houses out there, an agent has contact information for roughly 400 or 500 of their editors or publishers. However, of that number, the agents only deal with forty or fifty on a regular basis.

As agents often come out of the publishing industry itself, they have favorite houses and editors with whom they prefer to work. When they present material written by writers they represent, the agents typically go to the same editors each time. The relationships and friendships they establish get them in the door to present their writer's work.

Agents spend time building relationships with editors and publishers. Because of this, they have a much easier time getting hold of these folks and discussing an idea with them. Their foot in the door may boost an author's sales or get her into a publishing house that generally doesn't accept unsolicited or new authors.

An agent may work alone or be part of a large group of agents in one office. The lone agent typically has an office and works out of her home. The agency more than likely is a group of former editors or publishers who got together to form the agency and now represent many authors.

As a first time writer you may find yourself more welcome at a smaller or one-person agency. The large agencies don't often solicit or accept first-time authors and their manuscripts unless someone they know refers them. Writer's organizations and their websites indicate if an agency is accepting new authors or not (see the list of "Associations of Interest to Writers" elsewhere in this book).

Sometimes the agencies agree to look at your work or proposal if you can prove to them you have a book published and currently in print. If they think you have potential from what they see it can be a foot in the door to a professional relationship.

Typically an agent sends out multiple submissions to the houses they think would be interested in your book idea. It's not unheard of for an agent to send proposals to anywhere from three to fifteen houses all at one time. While most editors and publishers frown upon this practice, the agents would never get anything sold if they waited for each response (rejection) to come back.

The rejection rate, which no agents like to talk about, is, on average, twenty-five percent of the work presented. What I'm saying is that just because you have an agent doesn't mean she can sell your work to the first person who sees it — or at all for that matter.

How do you know if you should have an agent or not? In the publishing industry, it's generally accepted that if you write fiction (not short stories) you'll have an agent and if you write non-fiction, academic books, textbooks or poetry you won't have an agent. The reason being is that non-fiction makes less money up front and more over the long-term and fiction makes more up front than over the long-term. It isn't worth giving up a share of the profit to an agent for a non-fiction book.

Having an agent can have many advantages and disadvantages. If you feel your non-fiction book is a best seller that will make thousands of dollars for you then it may be worth considering a good agent to help you navigate the contract pitfalls unwary newcomers fall into. If your sales will be average, then an agent won't be able to help much. The trick is to consider all the facts and decide if you do or don't want (and need) an agent.

Any great agent can negotiate things into your contract that you either don't know about or won't be able to make happen. As agents deal with publishers and editors on a regular basis they know what the publishers consider important and what points they are willing to let go.

For example, an agent may be able to get a publisher to include you in the cover design/selection. If you have a good eye and a skill for design, this might be important to you. You'll know what makes a good cover and complements the copy. Most publishers would rather not include an author in this decision, but they may be willing to make a concession because of their respect for your agent.

Publishers believe marketing is vital to selling fiction and not so vital to selling non-fiction. An agent might be able to get the publisher to commit in writing how much and what they will do as far as marketing your book.

Budgets for marketing are set long before the book is written but obviously the more exposure a book gets the better it sells regardless of its genre. Sometimes an agent can convince the publisher to spend a little more on marketing and therefore increase sales and your commissions.

Another advantage to having an agent is their ability to unemotionally negotiate a better financial settlement for the writer. A publisher may be willing to go a little higher on the advance or the royalty percentage if they have a relationship they value with the agent.

Say, for example, two years ago the agent brought them an author who wrote a best-seller, they are inclined to invest more money in the writers that agent represents in hopes of having more successful authors backed by a proven agent join their team.

On the other hand, agents typically take ten to fifteen percent of whatever an author makes on the sale of the book. The norm is ten percent on domestic books and fifteen percent on international work. That, to me, in an industry that pays authors poorly, is an awful lot to part with. Particularly when, in my humble opinion, it's possible to do it yourself.

When selecting an agent you must ask if there are any other fees or charges for work performed. Some agents have a reader's fee, copyright fees, fees for manuscript typing, photocopying, long distance calls, etc. It's easy not to find this out until you get a bill in the mail from your agent.

Many of the agents listed in the *Writer's Market* or *The Writer's Handbook* specifically define what fees they do and don't charge. It's worth selecting one of these agents that clearly state what they charge in order to save your nickels and dimes, which add up fast.

Another thing to consider when searching for an author's representative is what, if any, particular field they specialize in. If an agent has been around for sometime and has a strong group of authors she represents she may find it lucrative and viable to narrow her focus to one genre. It may match your genre and work out well for both of you.

The publishing house automatically pays any earnings directly to your agent. The agent, who keeps your "books" for you, turns around and deducts his percentage from the amount received and writes you a check for the balance.

An agent often takes the hassle of presenting the manuscript off the author's hands, leaving the writer free to write or brainstorm for the next book. In effect, an agent removes some of the more mundane tasks an author deals with and allows the writer to do what she was meant to do — write.

As many writers are simply not very good at being organized or dealing with the minutiae of anything other than writing, the lifting of this burden gives them license to be creative full-time. There isn't any need to worry about non-writing details such as tracking commission payments, making copies or writing letters.

Depending on an agent's personality, he may not be very organized and may be more trouble than he is worth in helping the writer stay on top of deadlines and organizational issues. What I'd suggest is finding an agent with strengths that compliment your weaknesses. For example if you are solitary and reserved, the agent complements you if she is outgoing and congenial.

If you choose to go with an agent it may not be easy to find one. Many of the good ones already have enough writers to work with (typically they manage business affairs for fifty to 100 writers) and aren't taking on new clients. This is particularly true if you're looking for one located in the same city where the big publisher's offices are.

Those that work out of your hometown may not have as much of a rapport with the publishers as you would like. However, it might not be wise to rule out an agent just because they aren't based where the larger houses have their offices. These days there are so many means of staying in touch electronically and it is an acceptable way to do business.

One point that needs to be made here is that, as I said earlier, agents typically deal with the same publishing houses over and over again. They normally go to the bigger houses because they know the chances of making a sale are better due to the volume that publisher produces. Also, they realize the money and marketing efforts are likely to be better. Therefore, at a large house the publisher may hear from thirty agents and a small house hears from under ten.

Does this make the case for going to the smaller houses? It depends on your perspective. If you're a writer doing it on your own, then a smaller house that doesn't have as many agents knocking at it's door would be a better bet. However, if you have an agent you'll want her to contact as many houses as possible no matter what their size to increase the odds of a sale.

Some writers say agents should not be allowed to edit the writer's work, as they aren't editors. I tend to disagree. I think a good agent recognizes a good book idea and a well-written manuscript. Find an agent that does whatever you need them to do to facilitate a book that sells and reads well.

It's great to be able to talk to someone who understands the industry and can be very objective when presented with a book idea. You know your agent will be honest with her opinion and you can trust her to let you know if your concept is a bad one.

Finding a good agent with important industry contacts, a personality that is complementary to that of the author's and is not too busy to dedicate the necessary time to any one author may be worth considering.

On the flip side of your choosing an agent is the fact that an agent may not want to choose you. As there are thousands and thousands of would-be writers seeking representation by an agent, it allows the better agents to be selective. I wouldn't discourage you from trying to get on board with a stellar and seasoned agent, but if you are new to the world of publishing you may have a better chance with a newer agent or agency.

Those agents who are veterans often know each other from working with the same publishers or meeting for years at book fairs. If an agent turns you down but offers encouragement as to your potential as a writer, ask him or her to suggest another capable agent. If the first agent's dance card is full, she may be willing to give you a fellow agent's name and number.

I have found that picking up the phone and calling an agent or the agency they work for is a good way to get a feel for their way of doing business and their personality. If you call and end up liking them, they are pleasant to deal with and you think they like you then this may be someone you'd like to consider.

Be frank with whomever you speak with and let them know you are a new author looking for an agent. Find out how many books they have managed to sell and see if they'll tell you how well the books did. Also, inquire how long they have been in the industry and which houses they typically work with. You may even want to throw your book idea their way and see what happens. You'll quickly know if they are nasty or nice by they way they respond.

After that good first impression it's time to get down to more serious business and negotiate an arrangement. The agent may tell you they aren't taking on any new clients and it is up to you to convince them otherwise if you are certain they are the ones for you. If not, move on. Others will say they only accept new clients if they receive a query letter for a specific book idea. After having a satisfactory dialog it may be time to write that letter.

Publicists or Marketing Consultants

A publicist or marketing consultant may be another alternative to having an agent — particularly if you are writing non-fiction. A publicist is someone who doesn't go to the publisher to represent you or negotiate a contract for you. Rather, this person helps get you out into the public eye and helps you sell your books.

For example your publicist or marketing consultant, if he is any good, has contacts in various industries such as television and bookstores. He can set up interviews for you on the radio, book signings at the major outlets, speaking engagements at local events, book clubs, the library and appearances on television.

The publicists make the calls, sets the appointments and essentially market you and your book to anyone who is willing to talk to you. The actual appearance or interview is up to you to pull off in the best way you can. You must put your best foot forward and, of course, exude expertise in the book's subject.

If there is a current event taking place that captures the media's attention, it behooves your publicist to get you an appearance on any and all appropriate shows to shed light on whatever

35

the subject may be. For example, when the American Embassy in Kenya was bombed, had I had a publicist at the time, he should have called everyone in his database to get me to speak as an expert on Kenya. It may or may not have sold many of my books as it's a travel book, but any exposure is good and you never know where it can lead.

There are many places to find a publicist. First try an online search for literary agents. A good publicist should at least be able to set himself up on the Internet, either through an organization he belongs to or through his own website.

Another option is to try the resources available at your local library. For a list of potential names and contacts look for titles such as *Literary Market Place, Publisher's Weekly, Association of Author's Representatives (AAR), Writer's Market* and *The Yellow Pages*.

Perhaps a more conservative and less costly option is to go to your local college or university and talk to the professors in charge of the marketing, sales, communications or media courses/departments. They may be willing to take you on as a class project to see just how much exposure they can get for you.

If not, then these teachers can recommend a student with a marketing major to work for you as a publicist. The student probably needs the money and is willing to help to get credit or exposure. Remember however, this person won't have much experience and it could be a difficult road to travel.

At the large publishing houses there is one person or perhaps several people who have a hand in the publicity of your book. They may have varying titles such as publicist, marketing consultant, publicity director or special sales director but they all have the same directive — sell and market the book and the author.

If you feel that your publisher, particularly if it is a small company, isn't getting your book as much exposure as you think he should, talk to him and see if it's possible for you or your publicist to get involved. He may not want you sticking your nose into his marketing affairs, but if it helps sales, I don't think you'll hear a resounding "No," especially if you can present some sort of a plan.

36

3. SPECIFICATIONS

Should This Really Be a Book?

Once you make a written list of all the book ideas you think you would be good at writing and would like to write, it's time to delve deeper and determine if they really are worthy of becoming a book.

Looking at your list of ideas drafted on a legal pad can sometimes open your eyes to the fact that some of them need to be scrapped. They may seem strong initially, but under closer scrutiny they fall apart. And that's okay too, because your list is only the beginning and a necessary place to start.

If you are stuck about how to progress with your idea, walk away and put some time and distance between you and it. When you come back later to put some flesh on the bones of your work, subconsciously you'll find things progressed and the flow begins anew. It will be clearer to you whether you should scrap the idea or keep going.

On that legal pad, write down as many ideas and thoughts as you can that are relevant to the subject. If you end up with at least nine major categories with five substantial sub-categories under each one, it looks like you've got yourself an outline for a book.

Conversely, if there's too much information, think about doing a series of books. This is a great way to sell more than one book and can be very profitable. The most obvious advantage is the savings for a series can be huge in terms of marketing. It costs the same to market one book, as it does for a series of five.

Look around at the competition. If there are other books on the topic, it's likely that there is enough information to justify a book. Other books on the topic indicate positively there is a market for the subject and that publishers like it.

See what else is available on your subject by taking a trip to the library. Browse the newspapers, magazines, pamphlets and any other published materials you can get your hands on. Look for surveys, reports and statistics that support your idea for a weighty, full-length book.

During your research you may decide the idea you came up with is a good one but there isn't enough to fill a 200-page book. That's okay. It's better to know now than to sell the idea and be stuck trying to fill the pages, or to renege on your contract.

If your ideas shrink under examination, don't throw them out just yet. Think about them a little more and a new and fuller angle may come to you.

Perhaps, instead of a book, the idea warrants becoming a pamphlet, booklet or magazine article. Look around for someone who publishes these things or perhaps consider self-publishing. You can sell several thousand copies of your booklet for, let's say $7 each, and make a few bucks.

When trying to decide, book or booklet, sometimes it's easiest to sit down and write. If you write everything you know about a subject and you can only come up with 5,000 words you'll know to turn it into a booklet. If you have anywhere from 500 to 2,500 words and are coming up empty for more, then sell your writing as a magazine article.

For example, say you are a computer guru and work as a technician by day. Your book idea is to produce the most comprehensive book available, written in plain English, for anyone wanting to know the ins and outs of Wide Area Network (WAN). Your audience may be relatively small and not appeal to a large publisher. However, a specialized technical publishing house with this particular niche may jump at the chance to work with you to produce a large booklet or pamphlet. Or, perhaps a school that teaches technical courses is a potential buyer worth checking-out.

Once you determine the book has enough meat to fill it, then an important question to ask yourself is, is my book timely or time sensitive? You may have an awesome and innovative idea for a book the public desperately needs. Say for example, *How to Make Your Stock Market Portfolio Recession Proof.* This is a good idea right now, but twelve to eighteen months from now, once it's ready to sell, who knows, the market could be up and strong again. The risk of having such a time sensitive book simply won't win over many publishers.

Gathering the Content

Gathering information can be overwhelming. If you go about it systematically, everything eventually falls into place. The secret is to keep it organized and take small steps. If you look at the project as a whole, it's daunting and you will be intimidated. Many people get scared at this point and never go any further than dreaming about writing and getting a book published.

The way to deal with and beat this loser's syndrome is to use your outline/table of contents (see Chapter 7 for more on outlines). Pick one heading and write everything you know or can find on that one heading's subject. Then move on to the next one. Pretty soon you'll see flesh on the bones of your frame and before you know it, you have all the contents you need for a great book.

As you go along taking notes, ideas crop up that need to be included in a different chapter or under a different heading. Take the few seconds to find the appropriate heading and in large bold letters that catch your eye, jot a memory-jogger note to include whatever it was you thought important. Later you can come back and round the idea out.

One way to gain credentials and gather insights for your book is to get actual experience in the field you want to write about. If for example you want to write a book on how to start a mail-order business making and selling rubber stamps, start one and run it. Or perhaps you want to learn how to fly fish and eventually start a fly fishing school; do it. All the while taking copious notes and perhaps keeping a journal which eventually turns into one or more books.

But remember you don't have to be an expert and write everything from memory and/or experience. For most of us, that would probably mean we'd write one book at best in our lifetime. Publishers expect you as a writer to be proficient as a researcher too.

There are all kinds of ways and places to get and gather information. The research available to us as writers these days is fantastic. We can use the library, the Internet, The Library of Congress, commercial or private associations and organizations, and specialists and experts.

Interviews with experts can be a great source of information and quotes to boost your book's credibility and page count. These sources are usually forthcoming when they know they'll be quoted in the book. However, those that are more popular may only be willing to accept your interview for a fee. Before you dismiss the people that charge, bear in mind the better known your expert the more impressive your book is.

For example, if you can get Charleston Heston to give you an interview on his methods of trap and skeet shooting it makes sense that this boosts sales. If he supports and endorses the book, people who hate and love him will buy it.

Sometimes these experts have websites and e-mail they prefer as an initial point of contact. However, there's nothing wrong with using the phone. If the expert is interested, he'll be willing to talk. If not, then he'll give you that impression and you can move on to someone else.

If you know of a book author who wrote on the subject you are interested in, try getting in touch with him or her, preferably via e-mail. A good source for finding contact information on the Internet is www.anywho.com. Here, you are likely to find an address, e-mail address, website and/or phone number.

Using another author can be tricky if the two books have the same subject. But if you use the author to enhance only a specific section of your book there should be no conflict of interest.

Government organizations, agencies and universities often house experts in the most unlikely subjects and it's worth taking a look at their websites. Many such organizations have lists of available authorities locally and globally. Begin your search online by looking for broad government agencies that could possibly have the information you need and work your way down through the network to a narrower focus.

College papers, white papers and technical studies/findings that college students or professors write to gain their degree or tenure can be great sources for factual research applicable to your manuscript. These academics must write a thesis and often come up with unique and obscure ideas you can to use to support your argument or illustrate a point.

If fiction is what you're writing, these same sources apply to your effort as a fact-checking venue or for guidance on the credibility and correctness of your story. For example, if your villain is building a flying machine it might behoove you to check the facts on aerodynamics before you make the bad guy do something aeronautically impossible.

Most net users use the more common search engines such as Google, Yahoo!, Alta Vista or AskJeeves, to do a broad search for the topic in question. For the most part, the search engines give users more information than they can possibly use. However if the topic is unusual the search engines come up with little or nothing. There are other options on the Internet for finding data.

A few such places are electronic newsstands and mailing lists where thousands of newspapers, magazines and other media are listed by category, name or country. At these sites, you'll find how many magazines there are dedicated to readers of your subject. Perhaps you can use them for research material or find someone like the Editor-in-Chief to interview. Try www.newsdirectory.com, www.deja.com, http://infomine.ucr.edu, http://dir.lycos.com/Reference, or the *Encyclopedia of Associations* at www.dialog.com.

Databases are another source for finding information online. Sometimes the online databases offer more than the search engines because they take you to academic sources such as colleges and universities in the US and abroad. Tap in to the Library of Congress for their database of thousands of books, or try the databases at Lycos.com.

For lists of magazines as statistical resources, search The Writers Guidelines Database, Writer's Digest, The Electronic Journal Mine or The Market List (for fiction). See Chapter 4's section on "Market Statistics" for a more comprehensive list of additional web resources.

Some sites require you to subscribe or at least register to get in, but there are many others that are free. Don't dismiss the places that want you to subscribe or register too quickly. Instead look around the home page and see if they offer any links to other sites or sources that may be free.

If you are able to show in your proposal that you found ten sources who willingly lend themselves to your effort, all the better to show how meticulous and resolved you are to doing the job well. All the publishing house wants to be convinced of at this point is that you can actually put together a credible and ultimately a saleable product.

Always check on the copyrights and ownership of any material you want to use. If necessary, get permission and if that isn't forthcoming, don't use the data.

The ugliest word a writer hears is plagiarism. And boy, is it easy to fall into this trap when doing your research. It seems so innocent when you gather other books on the subject you're planning on writing about. The next thing you know, you've copied a sentence or paragraph verbatim. That's plagiarism. Copying can cost you financially and ruin your reputation. Besides, it makes you feel dirty to know the end product really wasn't yours.

What I prefer to do is to read other publications on the topic I'm interested in and jot down simple notes. All I'm looking for is ideas. Once these ideas are organized into some sort of order, I can begin writing. I compile all my notes, from all different sources to help me write an orderly and informative book in my own words and in my own style.

If you come across something you absolutely can't write in your own way or with your own touch, write and ask permission to reproduce the material. These requests are seldom turned down, especially if you give the proper credit.

How Many Chapters to Include

When writing a book proposal you want to impress your potential publisher by providing a comprehensive table of contents with a chapter-by-chapter outline. You want the editor to be convinced that there is clearly enough material for a book and that you are good enough to write it.

As a general rule of thumb, the average non-fiction book includes anywhere from eight to fifteen chapters. Anything less and the publishing house may decide there isn't enough material to warrant a book. To be on the safe side, try to come up with at least nine chapters if you can.

In a manuscript with 60,000 words you end up with 150 typeset pages (400 words per page). If you propose eight chapters, that translates into approximately nineteen pages per chapter — not a bad little book.

There isn't a right or wrong way to calculate how many chapters your book needs to cover the material. The number of chapters is determined by how long the book is and how many main headings it warrants. The longer the book the more chapters you'll need to break it down into manageable and readable portions.

In some books, usually fiction, you'll find a chapter with one page in it. This is for emphasis and works well in that genre. But in general I'd say no fewer than ten pages and no more than twenty-five per chapter.

You need to include chapter titles and a brief description of each chapter's contents in your book proposal. And at this point you'll have a good idea of how many chapters it breaks down into.

Here's what I included in my proposal for this book as my Chapter 3 outline:

Specifications
- Should this really be a book?
- Is there enough significant content?
- Working with publishers and making suggestions
- Determining how many chapters to include
- Calculating the number of pages
- Including sidebars, charts and photographs
- Deciding book size

Deciding Book Size

As a rough template to determine the length of a book — the number of final published pages — consider these guidelines. Bear in mind the calculations are imperfect and vary depending on the type size and the number of graphics, but they serve as a good general template.

The average, standard-size, non-fiction book is about 200 typeset pages. Each typeset page contains approximately 400 words. Therefore, a 200 page typeset book (with 400 words per page) equates to a double-spaced manuscript of 80,000 words. A double-spaced manuscript of 60,000 words ends up with approximately 150 typeset book pages. Of course your book may run anywhere from 36,000 to 200,000 words, depending on how much there is to write about and what the publisher's length requirements are.

Remember that costs are very important issues to a publishing house. They want to spend the least amount possible to produce the best conceivable book. The more pages you have in your book, the more it's going to cost to print, typeset and edit (in terms of man-hours). Conversely, though, the more books printed, the cheaper it is for the publisher. Try to find a good size-balance between too big to be of interest to the publisher and too small and not worth producing.

Another factor affecting the length of your book is the format. Often publishers have a particular style they use on all their books and are likely to want to stick to it. Sometimes, however, they don't specify any particular style and leave this up to you — at least initially. You can use this to your advantage to make your book proposal different (and eye-catching) from the competition, even if the publisher changes it later.

Whatever the competitive books look like, try to make yours different, or more attractive or easier to use. Take the format and work on several ways to break it into major sections or unique organizational schemes. This may appeal to the publisher you are pursuing and get you that sale.

Make your type larger so it's easier to read for older folks, or add more sub-headings to divide the book into more manageable parts. Try to organize your illustrations in a more interesting or user-friendly fashion. Add sidebars for quick reference and offer checklists to make your book interactive. Keep in mind, all these approaches take up more space than ordinary lines of text and add more pages to the overall book.

What with employment scarce, a volatile market and folks hanging out at home more, there may be extra dollars budgeted in households for the comfort found in books.

You might want to point out in your proposal one of two things — either you want to write a condensed (smaller) and less expensive paperback book because the readers don't have as much money. (This idea may appeal to a publisher because the book is less costly to produce.) Or, you want to write a big, expensive hardbound book. Since people aren't spending money traveling, they are willing to spend more gratifying themselves with a really lovely book they can treasure forever.

Length of the final product and how you propose it all depends on your subject, how you want to present it and what else is out there. But all the publishers expect at least 100 printed pages for a typical non-fiction book.

Trim size is the term used for the size of the final product once it's off the printing press and ready to ship to bookstores. In your proposal you need to suggest the size you think works best.

If you have no idea what to do here, go to a book outlet and find a book you think is the right size. Measure the book's dimensions — 6.75 inches in height and 4.25 inches in width, perhaps, with 12-point type — and suggest this as your final trim size. Again, this is only a suggested size and the publisher is likely to change it to whatever he thinks works best but it shows you know a little something and are considering every angle.

The most common sizes for books are 5-1/2 inches by 8-1/2 inches and 8-1/2 inches by 11 inches. Larger books or coffee-table publications are printed in special customized sizes and are usually hardcover. The smaller sizes are by far the most common, economical and easiest to handle for printing and distributing.

The term **signature** might be worth familiarizing yourself with in regards to determining size. A signature is an uncut booklet or collection of untrimmed pages that come off the press. Signatures are arranged in multiple page groups or "impose" (from the word imposition). Any number divisible by four, up to 128, is acceptable as the number of pages in a signature.

The easiest number to work with, and the number most commonly used, is thirty-two pages per signature. The number of pages in a signature depends on the size of the book and the size of the press running the job. The binding also has something to do with the number of pages in the signature.

In general, however, when calculating the number of pages to suggest to your publisher, decide you'll have any number of pages divisible by thirty-two. To print signatures of thirty-two pages is most cost effective for the publisher — 160 pages (five signatures), 256 pages (eight signatures) or 320 pages (ten signatures).

The first page of the main body of a book is called a recto page and always falls on the right hand side. Right hand pages are always odd folio (page) numbers. Books always have and always will have odd numbered pages when completed.

Frontmatter is pages that come in front of the actual body of the book. These pages vary significantly in number depending on what and how many the publishers want to include. Usually, they include a table of contents, title, copyrights, foreword, acknowledgements and dedication pages.

Backmatter is found in the last pages of a book but is not essential to all books. It's used as reference material and also referred to as "end matter." An appendix, notes, a glossary, an index, and a bibliography would be found in the backmatter.

One thing to consider during your page number calculation is the number of pages in the frontmatter and backmatter that aren't actually part of the manuscript. These pages may or may not carry a folio, but they are part of the total number of pages in the book and should be included in the calculation. You may not have any idea how many pages these sections needs, so what I suggest again is to find a book of the length you plan on writing, see how many front and back pages they used, and use that as your example.

Suggesting a Price Point

Book publishers already know how much it costs to produce a book of a particular size. They have a standard formula they follow to determine how many books they must print and how much they need to charge for each book in order to cover expenses and make a profit. That is what they are in business to do.

Hence, you might think your effort involved in determining a price may be futile but it won't be. It is a necessary exercise for both you and the publishing house. It shows the publisher you used your head and thought about how much your book is worth and how much richer your x percent royalty and advance is going to make you. It also lets you know what kind of money, if any, there is in it for you.

I know it may crush you to think they aren't too concerned about giving the reading public the best possible subject matter, but in reality that is probably their second goal. If they want to stay in business they must first make money and pay their bills. Then they can try to be the best they can be in terms of quality reading materials. In a perfect world, the writer and publisher achieve both objectives at the same time with each book.

Just as the publisher is concerned about money, so should you be. In this section of your proposal there are two different issues at hand. The first is calculating how much you think the book sells for and the second is determining what up-front costs you'll incur while writing the book.

Keep in mind that the expenses (per copy) incurred by the publisher go down as the number of books printed/shipped go up. It's good to know, for example, that it costs more per book to ship five books than it does to ship a box of twenty-four books.

Also, the more books that run on the printing press at one time, the cheaper it is per book. The more paper a printing company buys, the cheaper it is. Using the same logic, we know it takes less labor and set-up fees per copy to print, collate, bind and ship 5,000 books than it does for fifty.

I know this is a strange concept, but volume means great savings to the publisher. Therefore, if you are going to order books, try to buy as many as you think you can sell because it is less expensive for everyone.

On average, a paperback book sells from $10.95 to $12.95. A hardcover book sells for anywhere from $19.95 to $29.95 on up. Naturally, the more famous and popular the author, the higher the price.

Once again, take yourself off to the nearest bookstore or the Internet and research books of similar size and content to what you propose. Use these as references for what price you think is appropriate for your book. The proof is in the pudding or in this case sale of books off the shelf.

If this is your first book and the topic is expected to sell relatively well, I'd suggest an average but somewhat conservative price. I figure it's better to make money by selling lots of books at a lower price rather than a few books at higher prices.

When opting for a certain price range keep in mind you are asking the reader to give up both his money and his time. He must feel the investment is worthwhile or there won't be a sale. When you reach this point in putting together your proposal, take the time to calculate how much it's going to cost you to write the book.

For example, figure out how many interviews you'll include and how much the phone bill will be. Expenses for film and for developing that film are legitimate costs incurred and should be include in your calculations. If travel is involved in gathering your data, whether by car, bus, train or plane, that is a significant factor to include in determining how much you'll spend to produce the book.

When you add up the total for the costs, you may or may not want to include a breakdown or the dollar amount in your proposal. If the editor or publisher sees the costs as too high and can't cover them, it may force him to reject the book — even if he thinks it's a good idea. On the other hand, if you don't ask for an expense allowance you certainly won't get one.

The exercise of calculating your expenses is a good one no matter if you turn it in as part of the proposal or not. You will have a clear picture in your mind of what you'll spend and how many sold books it takes to break even. You might even have time to save the money if you know when you'll need it.

In addition, you'll be prepared to accept, negotiate or reject the publisher's offer based on the projected numbers in your budget. Only you can decide if you would write the book at a loss just to get it into print. Remember, when you have one under your belt, even at a loss, your perceived value as a writer increases dramatically.

Working with Publishers

If you are a new writer trying to get a foothold in the door of a publishing house by submitting a book proposal, remember that demanding anything or commanding they do it your way won't be helpful to your cause. Make suggestions only and try to phrase things delicately when necessary.

Large publishing houses have large staffs that perform many different responsibilities. The larger the house, the more staff there is and the more people to deal with as you move along the assembly line during your book's production process. However, the person you must befriend and stay pals with is the first person you spoke to and who expressed an interest in your manuscript. This person becomes your advocate on the inside.

Working with senior editors is important but often they don't get too involved unless major decisions need to be made or a crisis handled. The acquiring editor, or your editor, works with you deciding what chunks need to be cut from the book, what needs to be added and what needs to be re-written. In other words, your editor edits for flow, readability and structure.

If the house is large enough there may even be time for someone to double-check your facts for accuracy and see if the data is the most current. A proofreader and/or copyeditor does this. They correct grammar, check spelling and possibly review organizational flow. Most people think an editor copy-edits when he's editing but he doesn't. This is usually a separate function unless the house is a small one.

The managing editor oversees the entire project and supervises all the other personnel working on your manuscript. If any freelance editors or proofreaders are brought into the project, the managing editor manages them too.

The person who does the index for your book (if it's not you) is likely to be under the auspices of the managing editor as well.

The titles and corresponding duties tend to change from publisher to publisher, but the steps to produce a book remain constant no matter who does the work. Remember this organizational chart of publishing personnel may not exist at a small house.

Personality and human traits play a bigger role in the book proposal selection process than perhaps they should. If the editor who receives your proposal has a hangover or her boss refused to give her the day off, she may be angry and decide to toss out or reject most of the overwhelming stack on her desk.

If on the other hand, her boss just gave her a huge raise and told her she was getting an assistant, she may take delight in saying yes to the next great proposal she sees. I guess being human can be good or bad depending on how things are the moment your proposal arrives on the desk of the individual in question.

Predilection and taste can also play a significant role in whether your proposal makes the cut or not. If the editor prefers happy endings to sad ones or books about boys over books about girls these things may influence his decision. His areas of expertise have some influence. What I'm saying is that who is looking at your work may have a great deal to do with whether it gets chosen or not and less to do with how good your idea and presentation are.

This being said, the editors must still follow the strict guidelines set by the publishing house. They are experts in the book field and know what they need or are looking for (for the most part) to keep them in business.

Sidebars, Charts and Photographs

To break up the text of a book, it's important to include some sort of graphics. The most common are sidebars, charts, drawings and photos but that is not to say there aren't many other endless forms of graphics available. Imagination, an artist's talents, and budget are the only constraints.

A sidebar is described as any type of helpful tips or information set aside from the body of the text for quick reference. The sidebar can be a short story, a set of facts or a checklist complementing the particular issue discussed on that page or in that chapter.

The format for a sidebar is text of some sort with optional supportive drawings set apart by a border or a box. The text is presented in the form of a bulleted list, short factual sentences, statistics or a descriptive list with accompanying drawn symbols — just to mention a few.

A chart is usually a bar graph, a pie chart, a line graph or a table. For example to track the rise and fall of the stock market you could use a line graph with distinctly different looking lines for each time period covered.

Readers love sidebars because it makes the text more interesting and easier to read. If the reader can't get into the body of the book right then, sidebars give them a quick reference or feel of what's to come. Because of this, editors often request a certain number of sidebars to go with a particular length or kind of book.

Photographs or electronic images are also used to breakup text and can be reproduced in black and white or color. They make your book interesting by showing the places and people who are significant to your topic. And the images add reality and dimension to your story.

Black and white is significantly cheaper to produce than color and therefore is the first choice of most publishers. If you think your book must have color illustrations, say for a flower gardening book or a book on historic parks, mention it in your proposal so the editors know the costs involved.

Illustrations or drawings are also common as sidebars. These can be color or black and white and show something that would be difficult to say in words. For example, how to tie a knot. It's much easier to see the progressive drawings (if done well) rather than try to describe with words the step-by-step tying process. If possible include both the words and drawings so they complement each other and do a better job for the reader.

Illustrations are especially critical when it comes to children's books because all children's books have drawings. The size and detail of the artwork changes depending on the age group targeted. The younger the age the larger and more frequent the illustrations.

Mark Twain's adventure books of Tom Sawyer and Huckleberry Finn enjoyed by young teens, for example, may have only two or three black and white illustrations per chapter. Meanwhile, Beatrix Potter's Peter Rabbit books for ages four to six have full-page, color drawings on every page and only a few lines of text.

Reading lines and lines of text with no visual respite bores the reader's brain. Once the mind disengages and you've lost your reader you may not get him or her back. Of course, with novels you generally don't find, nor have the option of, using illustrations to hold a reader's attention. The novel must be fascinating in its content and story to keep the reader coming back.

Readers, no matter how much they like to do so, have other important or nagging things to do besides read. The distractions are mighty. Children, television, cooking, cleaning, working, running errands, traveling, sleeping and a million other things that take the reader away from your book. Therefore, it's critical it be as interesting and appealing (both in content and visually) as possible to keep them hooked.

At a seminar I took on how editors make magazine pages look interesting, the teacher said there should be something on each page to engage the reader's eye. It might be bold words, bullets, borders, indentations or anything breaking the monotony of text. The idea was to place a dollar bill anywhere on a page and have no block of type bigger than the bill. We can translate that on a lesser scale to books, particularly non-fiction.

If your publisher agrees to do the book in color, which is not very common because of the expense, it's easier to make the book visually interesting. However, if your book won't have color except on the cover (which is standard), any kind of lists, checklists, bold text, italic text, drawings, charts, black and white photos will work to breakup the pages.

When creating charts or drawings include them in the body of the manuscript itself if you can. For example, if you are introducing a pie chart to the chapter, use your word processing and computer capabilities to insert it into your text where you want it.

For the publisher's convenience, any graphic or illustration should be on a page of its own. This allows the publisher or graphic artist to more easily do whatever needs to be done to facilitate reproduction.

Once your illustration, photo, graphic or chart is on the page, label it. Start with Chart I, and keep numbering all of your graphics progressively throughout your book or the outline of your proposal. This keeps things orderly, manageable and facilitates compiling your index later on.

If it's not possible to insert the chart or graphic electronically into your proposal or manuscript, leave a blank page, or at the very least half a blank page. In the center of that space or page type in a label — Chart I or Chart V.

Say you have a photograph or drawing you need scanned by the publisher and inserted at a certain spot. Take the photo or drawing and clearly label it to match the label on the blank page in your proposal, i.e. Chart I or Chart V. The typesetter can then place the graphic in the correct location by matching up the two corresponding chart numbers.

One word of caution when doing this; don't write on the back of your photo or drawing unless you use a special "grease" pencil. If you use a regular pen, the writing is likely to bleed or scan through when the artwork is processed. What I suggest if you don't have a grease pencil is write your chart number on a smallish piece of paper and tape (using graphic artist's tape, which is less sticky and won't hurt the image) it to the bottom of your graphic.

If the artwork, graphics, illustrations or photos aren't yours, it's best to get permission from the original owner to use them. Sometimes these folks want to be paid but not infrequently they are happy to let you use their work if they get appropriate credit. In most instances, the publisher requires you, the author, to get permission in writing. He often expects you to take care of related payments also. I know, I know, life isn't fair.

Be very specific when negotiating your contract with the publisher and have everything in writing. Find out if it's your responsibility or not to provide graphics and photographs. But find this out up front rather than in the final contract.

With the larger houses it's unlikely they will ask you to find artwork because they are equipped with art libraries, staff and other resources for this purpose. If the subject matter is very specific, and it isn't available to them, then you may be required to provide it. Either way, they will work closely with you to find or create just the right graphics.

It's more likely for the smaller houses to ask you to provide any graphics you want to use for your book. If you can't find illustrations or photos or produce them yourself professionally, the publishers may accept a rough sketch from you and have an in-house graphic artist or artists make the final image from that.

For example, one of my books needed lots of maps. I can't draw maps so that eliminated one option. We couldn't reproduces maps directly from other sources as that would be plagiarizing. Therefore, I gave the publisher photo copies of the pertinent areas from an atlas. I made notes on the side of the maps with arrows pointing to essential names and places, and the in-house artists drew the maps. They sent the final versions to me for proofreading and we easily avoided the copyright infringements by creating our own maps from scratch using the copies for reference.

Be careful if you use someone else's work to create your own, use it only as a guideline. You don't want to get sued after your first book is in print.

During the book proposal stage of your publishing journey you obviously won't need to provide the graphics. What you must do is let the publisher know roughly how many and what kind you envision.

The publisher realizes that you can't say precisely how many drawings to include, but if you do your outline and research correctly you'll have a good idea of what should be included. This is also great preparation for when you start writing. You will know what you want and much of your legwork and foundation is done.

Illustrations and graphics are important because they help keep the reader engaged and captivated. In addition, they explain and complement what you are trying to say. The publisher, who always has a particular style in mind, takes many of these decisions out of your hands. Sometimes for cost containment, a publisher decides there is no need to include illustrations of any kind. I like to include as many graphics as I can but the publisher ultimately makes that final decision.

However, there's no harm in including bold subheadings to define the sections of the chapters, or making your chapter headings and style interesting using different fonts and typefaces.

4. THE MARKET

Defining the Potential Audience

To sell your book idea to an editor or publisher it's critical you justify your book proposal with statistics defining the potential audience. The more people interested in your subject, the more likely you are to make a sale. Millions of buyers would be the best possible target numbers but if you can show hundreds of thousands then you still have a very good opportunity for selling your book idea.

For example, in the news lately there is a great deal of discussion about the rise and fall of the small businesses. Whenever you turn around, someone is starting a new business or re-organizing it. Statistics from the federal government write that these small businesses are the backbone of our local economy.

According to research for an article I was selling some time ago, there are 250,000 new small businesses started each year and more than ten million small companies across the country. This, of course, may be changing as the poor economy weeds out the weak. But what a great potential audience for a book — you could cover everything from bookkeeping, security, advertising, merchandizing, sales, employee training, diversity, taxes, customer service and so on. It might even make a great book series.

The good news relative to potential markets for your book is that book sales are up. This is a positive fact to emphasize to any publisher. That's what they need to hear to encourage the continued production of potentially profitable publications including yours.

After September 11th, the national trend became of one staying close to home and focusing on family, friends and quality of life. My research for an article in *Shopping Center World* magazine on shopping and buying trends across the USA shows people began taking a look at what was around them and appreciating what they had.

The statistical evidence from my research also showed travel is down, which we all know by now. Such things as reading, games, hiking, self-help, self-awareness and crafts (and books on those subjects) are the hot-ticket according to the latest retail sales figures.

Experts say this reading/book trend continues to bring in the profits with book sales totaling $25 billion in 2001. According to figures released by the Association of American Publishers, paperbound sales rose 1.4 percent ($1.93 billion) in June 2002, and they predict sales will carry-on in this direction. This is another good point to make to any potential publisher.

There is also the peripheral-buyer factor to consider and present in your proposal. If your book is targeted toward a specific calculable audience of book buyers in your genre, that is your core market. This group is the readers your book is targeted toward.

However, as your book passes through the bookstores and is marketed to the core group, there may be others who come across it who can use it in some way but are not the target audience. These readers would not normally specifically search for the book or buy it. But may buy it if they see it on the shelf. They may purchase it for themselves or for someone they know. They are considered peripheral-buyers.

For example, say your book is for those laid off from their corporate jobs seeking ways to reinvent themselves and find a new career. They want to update their image and find employment in a new field. You will not only have the core market of the thousands of Americans who are unemployed, but you will also have those peripheral-buyers who are employed but interested in a career change and don't know what fields are hot or how to go about the metamorphosis they need.

Potential publishers are very interested to know your answer to the question, "Is the topic of your book something your potential readers feel passionate about?" If you can prove the answer to the passion question is yes, you have a good chance of grabbing someone's interest at a publishing house.

One example of a passionate audience involves dog owners in America. These people have always been and are becoming more and more passionate about their pooches (me included). Take a look on the Internet or in your local *Yellow Pages* to see how many doggie day care centers and "natural food" doggie bakeries are popping up all over the country. It's reaching epidemic proportions and the pet industry is cashing in by the truckload.

Take the time when putting "The Market" section of your proposal together to show the publisher or editor that you know your reader. You want to be intimately familiar with all three million of them. How, you might ask?

Well, pretend that instead of three million readers, there is only one. Get to know this person's mind and what she wants. Ask her if she will spend $12.95 for this book you're writing. If you find out she doesn't have the cash to spare or has it but won't part with it — your book just died. For example, if your proposed book is about helping those who hoard their money overcome this spending disorder, it's unlikely you'll have a great response.

It also stands to reason that it is very important that those you are trying to get to buy your book actually read and enjoy doing so. It would be useless for example to write a book on automobile racing as statistics and surveys show that of the sixty million people who attend these marathon events, very few frequent bookstores. They don't read much and don't often buy books.

As I said in Chapter Two, it's important to explain to the publisher why your potential audience and reading public should buy your book. In that section, I was showing you how to explain to the publisher in you proposal why your book is better.

In this section I want you to share in your proposal why the readers need your book. The two ideas (why it's better and why they should buy it) are closely related. Both issues explain that your book helps readers learn how to do something or be youthful, interesting, wealthy, smart, happy, healthy etc. They need it because they want to be entertained or learn a new skill and you can give it to them.

Market Statistics

Finding credible market statistics to support your book proposal is a very large part of the marketing component for your book idea. Take a look in your library, at bookstore magazine racks and on the Internet for any magazines or e-zines that have your topic as their subject matter.

When putting together my proposal for this book for example I said that according to the Census Bureau there are now 174 million working-age adults ages 18 to 64. Many of them dream of writing and publishing a book or know someone (peripheral buyers) who they would give the book to as a gift (another good market source as possible holiday stocking-stuffer if the book comes out just before Christmas).

I presented the fact that *Writer's Digest*, a leading magazine for writers, claims they market to more than 200,000 writers/ subscribers for expert writing instruction. That means there are 200,000 potential buyers for *Secrets of Getting Your Book Published*, and that's using only one source.

I explained that during my research I discovered there are 1,256 upcoming conferences across the country for writers. The topics and available seminars vary widely, with most covering "How to Write" rather than "How to Get Published." Based on my research, I showed the potential market for a good book with insider information on getting a book published is substantial.

One service, called Standard Rate and Data Service (SRDS), is widely used among people looking for magazine publishing statistics. If you go to their website, www.srds.com, you must subscribe to get any information. However, the SRDS is available at your library or you can call the company directly at 708-256-6067 or 800-851-7737 for more information.

If you are interested in the circulation or potential advertising sales information in any number of magazines, SRDS is the place to look. The statistics are broken down into different classification by type of magazine.

The whole point of using the SRDS is to find out how many magazines there are for any particular genre, hunting for example, and what their circulation is. The numbers of people subscribing to the publications then become potential buyers for your book on hunting.

Try to think like a sales person when you're putting together your marketing statistics. Use factual drama to emphasize your point. For example, if your book is about breast cancer, find the statistics that talk about how many men actually get and die from the disease each year. Most people think of breast cancer as an issue only affecting women. By illustrating your point using statistical figures and little known data, you make your point more quickly and more loudly.

As I mentioned earlier, whether you are gathering content or market statistics, you will use the Internet. You can use the standard search engines which most of us use on a daily basis, and you can try electronic newsstands and databases (see Chapter 3's section on "Gathering the Content.")

Online bookstores are another ample source of information to use as part of your market analysis. By going to Amazon.com or the Barnes & Noble Booksellers website you can determine what else is out there. If there are other books on your subject, it's a good indication that the book is popular with the reading public and boosts your presentation of the available marketing statistics.

Some writers buy the top ten most recent competing titles to analyze them more closely. You may not want to do this, either because you spend too much money or because you don't want to support the competition by purchasing their books.

With sites and databases like these you can prove to a potential publisher there are x number of people in the nation or the world who will read whatever your subject is and have the statistics to back up your claim.

Sources of Interest to Writers

The list on the following pages may be of some use to you as you begin your journey down the road to getting your book published. I hope these groups are a source of inspiration, data, marketing, research and encouragement.

American Booksellers Association, 828 South Broadway, Tarrytown, NY 10591. Phone: 914-591-2665. Internet: http://bookweb.org

American Society of Journalists and Authors, Inc., 1501 Broadway, Suite 302, New York, NY 10036. Phone: 212-997-0947. Internet: www.asja.org

www.anywho.com Find an address, e-mail address, website or phone number.

Association of American Publishers, Inc., 71 Fifth Avenue, New York, NY 10003. Phone: 212-255-0200. Internet: www.publishers.org

Association of American University Presses, 584 Broadway, New York, NY, 10012. Phone: 214-941-6610. Internet: aaup.uchicago.edu

Association of Booksellers for Children, 3900 Sumac Circle, Middleton, WI 53563. Phone: 800-421-1665. Internet: www.writerswrite.com

Associations and Organizations of Interest to Writers www.poewar.com/articles/associations.htm

Association of Author's Representatives (agents), P.O. Box 237201, Ansonia Station, New York, NY 10023. Internet: www.aar-online.org

www.AuthorsOnTheWeb.com Marketing and hosting site.

Book Fairs: An Exhibiting Guide for Publishers, www.parapublishing.com

Book Industry Study Group, Inc., www.bisg.org
Market and analysis of the industry and more resources.

Bookwire, www.bookwire.com Marketing and hosting site.

Bookzone, www.bookzone.com Portal to searchable publishing resources.

Christian Writers Guild, www.christianwritersguild.com Writers courses.

Dbusiness.com, www.dbusiness.com Submit free press releases.

Dramatists Guild of America, 1501 Broadway, Suite 701, New York, NY 10036. Phone: 212-398-9366, Ext. 11, Internet: www.dramatistsguild.com

Editor & Publisher, www.mediainfo.com Weekly magazine covering the newspaper industry in North America.

Horror Writers Association, www.horror.org.

InternetBookInfo, www.Internetbookinfo.com Internet Book Information Center.

Library of Congress Online Catalog, http://catalog.loc.gov/

Literary Market Place, www.literarymarketplace.com

Mystery Writers of America, 17 E. 47th Street, 6th Floor, New York, NY 10017. Phone: 212-888-8171. Internet: www.mysterywriters.org

National Association of Science Writers, P.O. Box 294, Greenlawn, NY 11740. Phone: 516-757-5664. Internet: www.nasw.org

National Writers Association, 3140 S. Peoria, #295, Aurora, CO 80014. Phone: 303-841-0246. Internet: www.nationalwriters.com Writers community.

National Writers Union, 113 University Place, 6th Floor, New

York, NY 10003. Phone: 212-254-0279. Internet: www.nwu.org

Publisher's Weekly, http://publishersweekly.reviewsnews.com
News source of book publishing.

Romance Writers of America, 3707 FM 1960 West, Suite
555, Houston, TX, 77068. Phone: 281-440-6885. Internet:
www.rwanational.com

Science Fiction and Fantasy Writers of America, 532 La Guardia
Place, #632, New York, NY 10012. Internet: www.sfwa.org

www.shawguides.com Find speaking engagements. Writers conferences.

Society of Children's Book Writers and Illustrators, 8271 Bev-
erly Boulevard, Los Angeles, CA 90048. Phone: 323-782-1010.
Internet: www.scbwi.org

Society of Professional Journalists, 16 S. Jackson Street, Green-
castle, IN 46135. Phone: 765-653-3333. Internet: http://spj.org

Submit It! Internet: www.submitit.com
Submission service for websites.

The Association of Authors, 19901 Burnt Mill Road, #2701, Jack-
sonville, FL 32256. Phone: 906-616-3013. Internet:
www.societyofauthors.org

The Authors Guild, Inc., 330 W. 42nd St., 29th Fl., New York, NY
10036. Phone: 212-563-5904. Internet: www.authorsguild.org

The Catalog of Catalogs, www.communicationcreativity.com/
catalog.html Find specialized catalogs for many subjects. Free
e-mail newsletter about publishing.

Garden Writers Association, 10210 Leatherleaf Court, Manassas
VA, 20111. Phone: 703-257-1032. Internet: www.gwaa.org

THE MARKET

The International Directory of Little Magazines and Small Presses, www.wwnorton.com/catalog/fall00/668578.htm

Catalogs
The Market List, www.marketlist.com
Resource for fiction writers.

The Playwrights' Center, 2301 Franklin Avenue E., Minneapolis, MN 55406. Phone: 612-332-7481. Internet: www.pwcenter.org

Writer's Digest, www.writersdigest.com

Writers Guild of America East and West, 555 W. 57th Street, New York, NY 10019. Phone: 212-767-7800. Internet: www.wgaeast.org
7000 W. 3rd Street, Los Angeles, CA 90048. Phone: 213-951-4000. Internet: www.wga.org

Writer's Handbook, www.writersservices.com/WrHandbook

Writer's Market, www.writersmarket.com

Databases
Infomine, http://infomine.ucr.edu/

Lycos, http://dir.lycos.com/Reference/

Encyclopedia of Associations, www.dialog.com

Bookstores
www.barnesandnoble.com

www.Amazon.com

Newsgroups
www.deja.com Discussion forums.

www.callihan.com/weblinks/refer.htm Web tutorials.

Mailing lists
www.listz.com

http://e-newsletters.internet.com/

http://www.topica.com/

http://www.coollist.com/

Experts
Associations and Organizations of Interest to Writers, www.poewar.com/articles/associations.htm

Zuzu Petals Literary resources, Organizations of Interest to Poets and Writers, www.zuzu.com/wrt-org.htm

Markets/Database
Writer's Guidelines Database, www.writerswrite.com/guidelines

Writer's Digest, www.writersdigest.com

The Electronic Journal Mine, http://ejournal.coalliance.org

www.newsdirectory.com Magazine database.

Standard Rate and Data Service, www.srds.com
Magazine publishing statistics.

Small or Niche Publishing Houses
In general I would say writers overwhelmingly want to target their books to the larger houses in the publishing industry. They may feel it's more prestigious to be published by a "biggie," and that there is a better chance to make larger sums of money. All these things are probably true. However, it's my experience that the big guys are more likely to reject book ideas because of the volume of proposals they have to choose from.

Recently, *The Washington Post* dubbed independent publishing a "bright and vital spot" in "this illiterate culture," pointing out that niche publishers are succeeding where others failed by closely targeting books to specific audiences.

There certainly isn't any harm in trying to get in with the big houses as long as you are prepared to wait for replies and be rejected more often than not. However, for someone just starting out, I'd recommend going for the smaller and/or niche publishers.

A small publisher is just that — small and handles a lower volume of new books each year — but often open to a variety of subjects. A niche publisher, on the other hand, focuses on one or maybe two particular types of books. For example, a small house might print a book on walking to stay healthy and a book on fly-fishing in the same season. In contrast, a niche publisher would only work on a particular genre, like travel books or science fiction.

Niche publishers are thriving because their known audiences purchase the kinds of books they produce. These businesses figure out what particular groups of people, in very large numbers, like to read and feed them what they want. The Book Industry Study Group says such publishers "could represent a $14 billion market."

An advantage of going with a smaller house is that they are less likely, due to lack of manpower, to change your manuscript a great deal. This is good and bad depending on your point of view. If you aren't such a great writer, you may want all the editing and re-writing help you can get. But if you feel you're a proficient writer and editors change your material — well let's just say it can be most irritating.

Of course, how much and what gets changed varies from house to house and editor to editor. Each editor, copyeditor and proofreader is as different in his methods of editing and proofing as they are different in personality. The mechanics and procedures of doing the job are standard but the employees are all different in how far they take the job.

When an editor is editing a piece of work, I believe he or she should leave as much as possible intact. The things he or she should change are grammar, spelling, and organization if necessary, but very little else. Otherwise, in my opinion, the voice and personality of the writer is lost. The work turns into the product of the editor.

If the work needs that much re-writing and re-organizing because it isn't clear or well done, then that writer shouldn't have been hired in the first place. Whether or not a publisher likes a writer's characteristics and style should be determined way up front in the process.

Is the Market National and/or International?

You want to define your readership for the publisher in editorial as well as informational terms. By **editorial terms** I mean all the specifications of the book such as size, price, etc. as addressed in Chapter 3. By **informational terms** I mean what kind of language idiosyncrasies your readers demand that are common to their culture. If your book is strictly American, use American terminology and spelling. For example, use the term *corn* instead of *maize*.

If you plan on selling your book to international markets, presumably European/British, as well as American, define the terms doubly. For example, it is important to clarify for the readers such things as temperature and MPH for both continents — 95 degrees Fahrenheit [35 degrees Celsius], or 60 miles per hour [100 kilometers per hour].

Speaking of the international market, it might be worth mentioning *The International Directory of Little Magazines and Small Presses* here. We know that trends often start overseas and eventually end up in this country. If you want to be ready to write a book about hobbies, health issues, pastimes or beginning trends, you can try to get a jump on the rest of us authors by following what the international magazines and small presses write about.

The downside, of course, is that it's too much of a gamble. Whatever their trend is, it may never take off here, or if it does, you'll have to be the one to get it going (and that is a tough sell to any publisher).

A Worthwhile Effort

As I mentioned earlier, a publisher wants to feel comfortable with the fact that he can at least sell the first run of any book the house backs. If they don't think they can market enough copies to make a small profit and/or cover expenses, chances are they won't pursue your book.

The set-up costs for printing remain constant whether the number of items being printed is one or one million. It still costs x number of dollars for all the pre-press preparation and labor. The fluctuating price of paper may affect the post set-up costs but the expense of binding and printing remains relatively steady.

The first print run for a book (particularly through a smaller house) is typically 5,000. There is no reason to believe, however, that if a publishing house thinks it can sell a larger number of books, the print run shouldn't be 10,000 or 100,000.

If this is your first book and the publisher doesn't see it as a runaway best seller, chances are the press run will again be 5,000. You can probably count on making the advance and maybe a little more, but not much. This industry is well known for it's starving writers.

Once you get involved in the industry, you'll learn that just because a sticker is glued to your book showing one price doesn't mean it must be sold at that price. Often it is sold for much less. The discount schedule offered by all publishers is a sliding scale of reduced prices offered to the different kinds of buyers. The purpose of the discount schedule is to encourage bulk or volume books sales. In other words, the more books ordered by a book-seller, the cheaper the price they pay. A very large seller can get up to 50 percent knocked off the price. Libraries, small book-stores, schools, large booksellers and wholesalers each get the books at a different cost.

For the author, this could mean more books sold because they are cheaper. The effects show in the royalties paid out to you. If your contract stipulates you are to be paid on the price set for the book regardless of how much it sells for then it's good for you. However, if your contract reads the royalties are paid on the actual sales price of the book and the books sell at a discount because the bookseller bought them at a discount, your royalty goes down.

These intricate industry methods of operation can hurt the publisher just as much as the author. If the publishing house collects 100 percent of the sales price set for the book, it obviously does better than if it sells the book at a discount. Remember that the publisher then has to take that income and subtract the expenses of office overhead, manufacturing costs and royalties, which usually leaves a conservative profit for the house.

The accomplishment of being published by an honest-to-goodness publisher is often enough for many authors. They feel they have arrived and that the effort was worthwhile. Only you can decide how you feel about that.

Anyone that meets you, the author, from that point forward views you from a different perspective. Friends and family will never look at you quite the same way again. In essence, you become a mini-somebody and to many this is what it's all about.

Those who achieve author status but aren't making enough to live on from their books commonly supplement their incomes by teaching, freelancing articles to magazines, giving speeches and seminars or having a "regular" job on the side. Taking this course of action allows a writer to write and at the same time put food on the table. But it does mean giving up lots of evenings, weekends and sleeping-in to chase the dream.

For some book authors the doors begin to open as soon as their book is released. The topic of their book or the fact they are published gets them into all kinds of places they wouldn't normally be invited. For example, they may be sought after and offered free gifts, meals, travel, accommodations and products for appearing at an event, speaking to a group or teaching. This can be a fun and fairly lucrative option for any writer in the right arena.

Another angle that may make this worth the effort for you as a published author is the tax advantage. As long as you are actually in the business and set yourself up as a legitimate enterprise you may be able to claim deductions for your home office, the supplies you purchase and any expenses you incur while pursuing your occupation.

The Internal Revenue Service (IRS) has specific guidelines pertinent to what can and can't be deducted. Their rules even dictate what percentage of certain items can legitimately be claimed for such things as travel, utilities, car mileage and communication expenses.

As a writer with a small business you become prone to an audit, so be careful to follow the rules closely. If there's any doubt about what you're deducting, seek the advice of a professional. This is especially true as the tax laws and forms change constantly.

The bottom line and the harsh realities are that few authors make a killing in the world of book publishing. But the money must be acceptable to somebody or the industry (writers, publishers and sellers) wouldn't continue to survive and moderately flourish. But I think the truth is we all love what we do no matter what.

Reader's Report

What is a reader's report? It's exactly what its name suggests — someone who reads your work gives a report as to its worth, technical validity and the correctness of its contents. A reader's report is something publishers use or should use to cover their behinds.

The process isn't used on every new book going through the publishing house but is a good tool to ensure the facts are correct in the manuscript. Basically, the editor hires an outside expert or panel of experts in the book's field to check for accuracy and completeness.

If the book is about the how to systematically build a steam engine, it stands to reason someone who understands and has actually built one, should check to see the critical nuts and bolts are all being placed in the correct holes. An editor can't necessarily do that, and the publishing house can't employ fulltime experts unless they are publishing specialists.

An editor has many functions, including babysitting the author, keeping track of the production schedule, working with the marketing department, weeding through submissions, being a cheerleader and editing and suggesting manuscript improvements. In addition to all these tasks the editor finds and temporarily contracts an authority in the appropriate field to review a book for technical precision.

When an editor or publisher receives your book proposal,

he may be interested in working with you. But first, he needs to ascertain if you really know what you're talking about. This is also a good time for them to send the proposal to a specialist (or a group of specialists) for a reader's report.

The report can take many different forms. A standard form or set of questions is sometimes given to the reviewers by the publishing house. Having this checklist or guide makes the review process less difficult and time consuming for the experts. At other times the specialist must write a report himself — it can be anywhere from one to five pages long.

If a proposal or manuscript needs to go through this process, you can expect to add anywhere from four to eight weeks to the publishing process. Sometimes the people doing the review are in different locations and/or reviewing independently of one another.

According to the publishing industry, in order for a manuscript or proposal to be properly evaluated using a reader's report, there should be at least two readers. The editor naturally looks for experts who are willing to share their evaluation fairly, quickly and succinctly. They want someone who is somewhere between the Grinch and Mary Poppins; people who will share their evaluation fairly, quickly and succinctly. From the reports, an editor decides if she wants to pursue the project or not and if so, what to change or edit.

In many of the larger publishing houses a junior staff member produces another type of reader's report to determine the viability of the book not from the point of view of technical correctness, but rather from the marketability and potential popularity of the title.

This staff person reads the copy and reports on the quality of the writing, the import of the contents, the significance of the work and finally the market potential. She makes notes and comments on what is good or inferior in the potential manuscript and recommends either rejection or further consideration. This report, along with the author's pages, gets passed along to another level of editor or editors. He, or they, review(s) the reader's report from the junior staffer and then proceeds to do his or her own critique.

THE MARKET

As you can see, there are many people with varied opinions, personalities and points of view that affect your book. You may think it's factually correct and then you get someone whose point of view differs and you lose the sale. There's not much you can do about it except write the best book you can and hope it is good enough to pass muster with the critics.

5. COMPETITION

Why Do I Need to List the Competition?

In the "competition" section of your book proposal, your research is fairly simple. You find any books that compete directly or very closely with your topic that were published within the last five years.

Tracking down the competition and doing the research for your book proposal saves the publisher a whole lot of time. If the publishers had to do this kind of digging for each book idea they think might be worth producing, their overhead would go through the roof. They would need so many people they probably couldn't afford to operate. In addition, your effort tells them you are serious about doing the job right. You could look at this research, in part, as a test of you credibility.

Think of your proposal as a sales pitch in writing where your physical presence isn't allowed. You certainly want to make the presentation the very best it can be in order to sell the book idea without the benefit of being there to explain something or answer questions. Understanding this you can see why carefully tracking down, evaluating and presenting the competing publications to the publisher is imperative to success.

The competing books you list are very important to the publisher because this information is used to help decide if there is or isn't room for one more book on your proposed topic. Generally, if you find there are seven or more recent books on the subject, publishers tend to shy away from producing another one. If the number of competitors is anywhere between two and six, the odds just went up of your selling them you book idea. However, this is simply a guideline. I sold books that had plenty of competition, simply because my idea and angle were better or because the competition wasn't recently published or the publisher simply liked my concept and presentation. So if you really think you are on to something, go for it.

Where to Find the Competition

The details you'll need to collect on each competing book must include the title, the author, the publisher, the year of publication, the number of pages, the price and the format (by format in this instance I mean whether the book is paperback or hardbound). It's also helpful to your sale if you include the selection of graphics or illustrations the book contains or their lack thereof. Basically, you want to give the potential publisher a cliff-notes version of the books available.

Take a pad of paper with you to the library and write down the pertinent information as you find it. This is awkward but necessary as most of the books you'll be using are research books and cannot be checked-out. This is primarily true if you are doing research for a non-fiction book. Instead of taking the time to write down what you need, you may want to make a photocopy if you can, which helps avoid any errors. Or, take your laptop computer with you and type the data directly from the book into your proposal — that's a good timesaver.

One great source for finding the competition is a book entitled *Books In Print* (R.R. Bowker Company). It's an alphabetical listing of all books in print — roughly 600,000 of them. Listed are titles, publishers and authors of any book copyrighted including academic and scholarly works and technical publications. Find "The Subject Guide to Books in Print" subheading and look for the subject matter that interests you.

Another great place — perhaps the most up-to-date sources — are the Internet and the bookstores online. Amazon.com (www.amazon.com) and Barnes and Noble Booksellers (www.barnesandnoble.com) have sites that can be searched by subject. Once you arrive at these websites it's simply a matter of searching for your topic and writing down or cutting and pasting the pertinent information into your proposal. The books appearing here are more likely to be under five years old, but not always.

Including Essential Details on the Competition

With every book you find that competes with yours, it's important that you emphasize why your book is different and better. Come up with one or two mid-length paragraphs describing those distinctions and improvements in all aspects of the book, such as contents, style, graphics and length.

Try not to bash the competing book too badly as it may give a negative impression about you. You want to be diplomatic and tactful when trying to say their book stinks and yours won't. This is very difficult to do with grace, so it's better to be factual and to the point without using too many unflattering adjectives.

I remember one rejection letter I got from a publisher that was just downright nasty! Apparently he felt I was too harsh when detailing the competing travel books on Belize. He told me in no uncertain terms there was no way I could do a better job and that he felt the author covered the country well. He said there was no need for yet another book when the ones in print were effective. I was crushed. But finally I decided to see the bright side — at least he read my proposal!

Included in my proposal for this book I said, "The competition *Secrets of Getting Your Book Published* faces and which I encountered during my research was healthy enough to show there is a market for this kind of how-to book. The potential marketplace was not saturated with like-books, which would make one more overkill." Then I included the list of competitive titles and the pertinent information.

I explained the directly competing books were not as carefully organized as they should be. In addition, I said, they often left out what I consider to be vital information such as certain aspects of searching out the competition (graphics, and style) and market research.

I went on to say that, interestingly there were many more how-to-write books and self-publishing books than how-to-get-published books, available on the market.

Then I summarized what I found regarding price, "all but one were more than $14.99 and well over 200 pages. This leads me to conclude there is a need for a less expensive and smaller guide to getting published."

Competition Format

Following is how I listed the competition for my proposal on a Belize travel guide. It's a great format to follow when you put together your list of competing books.

Competition for Traveling to Belize

I. **The Adventure Guide to Belize by Harry S. Pariser. 2nd edition. Published by Hunter Publishing, Inc. 1992. 276 pages. $12.95. Paperback.**

This book is on the long side. The author has done a good job of covering most of Belize but does not include any maps. Belize is changing so fast this book is somewhat outdated. This publication includes a guide to Guatemala and Honduras which is far too much territory to cover in one vacation or one book...

2. **Belize Guide by Paul Glassman. Published by Passport Press, 1991. 281 pages. $13.95. Paperback.**

There are no color pictures to add interest to this book. Published in 1991, the information is outdated considering how fast Belize grows and changes. Guatemala is included in this Belize guidebook which doesn't do justice to either country.

A Look at Self-Publishing

With the proliferation of computers, self-publishing is relatively easy. It has become the outlet for many writers who are frustrated with trying to get a book into traditional print through traditional publishers.

Be comforted by the fact there are many distinguished and venerable authors who began the journey to fame by self-publishing. These writers couldn't get anyone to give them the time of day and lived in the world of rejection. See if you recognize any of these names: Carl Sandburg, Ezra Pound, James Joyce, Virginia Woolf, T.S. Eliot, Henry Thoreau, William Blake, Robert Burns, Walt Whitman, Zane Grey and Mark Twain.

As I see it, there are two fundamental reasons for wanting

to self-publish. The first and most obvious is to actually get published and avoid those nasty rejection letters. The second is to put more of the profit in your pocket as opposed to the pocket of a publishing house. Self-publishing, however, is a very rocky and daunting road so be cautious before you take the plunge.

Remember that no matter how smart and fabulous you are as a person and no matter how well respected, being self-published doesn't have much authority behind it. Your self-published work brings to the table only the respect you command from those who know you.

It might make you feel good to self-publish, and it should, but to have a publisher buy your book, out of thousands and thousands, is an even more tremendous accomplishment. Essentially someone who has absolutely no reason to ever want to know you gave your idea and work approval, validation and hence, credibility.

In the simplest of terms, the steps to being self-published are as follows: you decide what to write about, you sit down and draft your manuscript, you find someone to create a website if you can't do it, and you put your book up on the Internet. And there you have it — self-published (albeit electronically) you are!

The word self-publishing means different things to different people. You can produce the book for yourself and your immediate family. You can put it together as a one-time deal and spend your own capital (which you aren't likely to recuperate) to get it printed and on the market. Or you can set up a publishing business and produce your own book in addition to others and maybe make some money.

If all you want to do is write and sell your book to family and friends then by all means do so. Write it and have seventy-five copies printed and bound at your local print shop. You might make a few bucks or give it as a Christmas or birthday gift.

Just about everyone these days has a computer, which makes the actual writing process effortless in contrast to the archaic way of using a typewriter and carbon paper, or paper and ink, or a stylus and parchment! All that's required is to type and instantly edit or correct at your leisure.

In the old days you had to be a true craftsman (and maybe

even a masochist) to want to re-type or re-write pages over and over again each time you needed to add a sentence or paragraph or make typographical corrections.

Perhaps the down side of the electronic age is the easy access to computer word processing software and the proliferation of written materials. This has inundated publishers, making their work and the work of serious writers far tougher. There is too much to choose from because of the ease with which it's produced. And much of it isn't that good.

Because of this abundance of manuscripts, self-publishing is more and more popular. People want their work in print and won't take "No" for an answer — even if it means doing it themselves. This route can be profitable. More often than not, it isn't.

Once upon a time, producing a book was looked upon as impossible for anyone not involved and trained in the publishing industry. It was believed authors simply didn't posses the skills or perhaps even the learning ability to do so. The general impression was that an "artist" (that's how a writer was viewed) couldn't possibly have the stamina and self-discipline to produce his own publications. How things have changed.

Perhaps the most daunting facet of self-publishing is the financing. There is of course be a financial commitment on your part. To set yourself up as a legitimate company you incur initial expense for licenses, stationary, communication equipment and other business necessities.

For each book you decide to print professionally you can expect to spend approximately $20,000. In other words you'll have to put money out before you can start taking it in with sales. And in most instances it takes much more than one book to make a publisher or self-publisher financially successful.

The decisions made by a modern publisher, which you are if you go the self-publishing route, include equipment and production basics, size and specifications, editing and design, printer selection, pricing and discounting, compiling and carrying out a marketing plan, promotion and distribution.

Writing the book is actually only a small part of what it takes to self-publish. In addition to the writing and production you must be prepared to spend a considerable amount of time direct marketing and promoting.

You must also consider industry statistics which indicate that, of all the genres, non-fiction is the most likely to be successful through self-publishing because those types of books are less difficult to sell. Novels, children's books, poetry and fiction are harder to market and are seldom bought by bookstores directly from an author or self-publisher.

The good news about self-publishing is that you can do what you can yourself and then hire the professional help you need in the areas you aren't comfortable with, providing you have the cash or credit to do so. For anything you can't or won't do, there is someone out there that can and will do it, for a fee.

There are many freelancers in the publishing world that provide editing, proofreading, copyediting, illustrating, typesetting, marketing and printing; all for approximately the same prices that a larger publishing house gets. It may take some negotiating, but it has been done before and you can do it again. In any event, if you hire any of these folks, don't be afraid to negotiate and get the best deal you can.

More opportunities and advice exist in the self-publishing arena than is possible to cover in this book. However, there are many great reference books out there, such as *The Complete Guide to Successful Publishing* (Union Square Publishing), *How To Get Happily Published* (Harper Collins), *Literary Market Place*, *American Book Trade Directory*, and *Publishers Marketing Association*. In these works, you'll find the details of how to manage as you scramble down the self-publishing playing field.

Publisher's Weekly

Look for a journal publication entitled *Publisher's Weekly*. This is what most people in publishing read to keep track of who's who and what's new in their field. It may not lead you directly to the competition, but it helps you see what is in the minds of those in the publishing arena.

This bible of the book trade allows for communication between publishers of books, magazines and newspapers. If anything important occurs in the industry you are sure to read about it here.

The publication's unique and relatively small circulation belies the power it holds. It has little or no competition, which puts it in a dominant position right off the bat. In addition, the journal commands respect among industry insiders and therefore elicits direct or indirect reactions to its discourse.

Any editor who works with an author or a subject matter that comes up in PW will naturally influence others in the field to find a writer of their own to cover the same topic. For example, if PW touts a stream of books covering personal finance, you can be sure the message to other publishers is received loud and clear. If such an influential journal notices what the big items on a prevalent publisher's list are then others should follow suit and welcome books of this flavor or type as well.

Editors, agents and publishers are often asked to participate in the publication by doing interviews, offering commentary and generally giving insight into the soul of the publishing universe. This can help you follow a particular editor's likes, dislikes and perhaps give you enough information to get to know the editor.

In addition to the industry news, PW covers what titles are likely to appear over the coming year. You may not be able to find these lists/titles anywhere else as they are not in print yet, but still on the drawing board.

If you see any competing titles to your book idea listed, it may give you the edge when selling your work. For example, if you see a big publishing house has a new title on terrorism coming out in the next year, you may be able to use that as leverage with that house's competitor to sell your own book proposal on terrorism.

Publisher's Weekly is viewed by some as the *People* magazine of the publishing industry. When an editor leaves one publishing house and accepts a job at another house it often makes it into the "News and People" section of the journal.

This might be an opportune moment for you to present your proposal to the new editor as he may be open and welcoming to any new author willing to build a relationship. Not only is the editor vulnerable, but he needs to rebuild his stable of authors because writers are usually left behind with the old employer.

Whether you are self-publishing or being published through

a traditional publishing house, it's wise to send a review copy of your book to *Publisher's Weekly* (249 West 17th Street, New York, NY 10011, 212-463-6758, www.publishersweekly.com).

They should receive the review copy at least three months before its official publication date in order for it to have a chance at getting mentioned in the journal. Of course, there is no guarantee your book will get named, much less looked at, but it's worth a try. You never know what can happen and if they don't get a copy, it's guaranteed it won't be reviewed.

A subscription to *Publisher's Weekly* is costly ($189.00), but don't give up hope. Your local librarian probably subscribes, as this is what she and her employees use to see what books are about to come out. They use the publication to select what new books the library should buy for the coming season depending on what their budget allows. If the journal isn't on the library's shelf, ask to see their copy or they can tell you which library carries a copy.

How-to and Non-fiction Book Proposals

How-to and non-fiction books are designed to enrich readers' lives. There is a constant and tremendous demand from the public for books to improve them or their living in some way. I believe that we as a society are obsessed with wanting to know more or do better and we are able to do just that by reading and applying what we've learned from an expert.

Everyone we know has bought a book or been given the gift of a book at some time in their life that saved them money, helped them relax, taught them to do something, made them healthier and happier, and promised to change their life in some positive way.

My disposition and writing style lends itself more to this kind of writing as opposed to fiction. I think you will find your personality and interests dictate what kind of books you write also.

Steven King, the king of horror and fiction books, for example, started in school at a young age writing a satirical newsletter called *The Village Vomit!* Don't worry if your imagination isn't filled with unusual and wild ideas, as non-fiction can be profitable and fun to write too.

Naturally, you'll want to write something that sells. The secret is to come up with an idea that hasn't been done yet (is there such a thing?) and that there is a large market for. A tall order any time but it happens every year. You probably kick yourself and wonder why you didn't think of it first when you notice the trendy new book titles at the bookstore.

Recreational and sports books continue to be wildly popular. The X and Y generations, particularly, are into radical and extreme sports. They love to read about how it's done, what the new trends are and who is leading the pack. The hard part for the writer is to get there with her book first.

Character profiles or biographies seem to always be an instant hit. For some reason average people have a fascination with characters in history or the real world that achieve notoriety or infamy. A large portion of the reading population lives vicariously through the adventures of others and is captivated by the narrative.

Child rearing, parenting and books on babies historically sell and are a standard success in publishing. Anyone with a child seeks guidance and advice on how to do everything — feed, clothe, educate and discipline their children.

Books that are mainly photographic in nature also prove themselves to be profitable and popular. Regardless of age, people love to look at picture books. The good thing about a book of this type is that it's relatively quick to produce from the writer's standpoint. If you are a writer and a photographer so much the better. If not, team up with someone who has the skills you don't and find a unique subject that photographs well. The possibilities are endless — houses, people, places, boats, cars, animals, trees and anything else you can think of with a twist.

The enormous success of home improvement television shows is a clear indicator that anything to do with the home or garden is trendy at the moment. Can you decorate, fix a toilet, paint, weave, accessorize, color-coordinate, tile, cook, bake, arrange flowers, graft trees or organize a closet? If so, there are a million ideas here for a book and a million dollars worth of potential sales for it.

Inspirational and religious books are perhaps the best selling books ever to be published. Don't let the word religious put you off. This genre absolutely does not have to be preachy or pushy but instead makes the reader feel inspired or informs the reader how to accomplish a "higher" goal.

Take a trip to your local Christian or religious bookstore and you'll be surprised to find hundreds of books for sale. Traditionally, these types of books stay on the self for longer and often make more money for the author because of it.

Financial and money management books are always sought out because humans always want to be financially independent and secure. These types of subjects are harder to write because the topic is much more difficult than most. Therefore, a well-written guide to any kind of finances is easier to sell to a publisher exactly because it's harder to write and not as common.

To make your non-fiction book different and appealing to an editor, you might want to try the same old topics but with a new slant. You could write finance guidelines or inspirational books specifically geared to senior citizens. Not only will seniors buy the book, but also others (peripheral markets) will purchase it for their older mother, uncle, grandmother or friend.

In general, publishers are always looking for humorous book ideas. Humor is in high demand because it sells well and because skillfully written humor is hard to find.

If humor is your talent you should consider writing a book with a twist. Cover a normally serious topic and spin the funny side of it. For example, the title could be *Fifty Curious Tricks to Cheer a Sick Child*. I'm sure you get the idea.

The examples I mention are just a few of the better selling and more popular non-fiction book types. Let your imagination, research and observations find the niche you belong in. Continue to read, visit the library, study the bookshelves, pay attention to what's around you, join a club and have an open mind, the ideas will come to you.

Fiction Book Proposals

The rules of engagement vary somewhat when it comes to the different genres of writing. This truth is extended to book proposals also. For fiction, your proposal needs to be slightly altered from that of the non-fiction proposal.

As part of your fiction proposal, write a terrific cover letter and come up with separate sections including a title page, summary, specifications, a look at the potential market, promotion ideas and author's bio — all of the collective segments you should also submit for a non-fiction proposal.

Instead of a table of contents necessary for non-fiction, you need to write anywhere from ten to twenty pages summarizing your story. This belongs in the summary section. Here's your chance to layout the plot, introduce your main characters, define the conflict and explain the resolution.

You must enclose two sample chapters. In my opinion, one should be the first and opening chapter where the main players are introduced and the plot is unveiled. The second can be any other chapter full of well-written drama and exciting action that hooks the reader.

One writer I know sent in snippets from five or six chapters. The editor was kind enough to send a rejection letter with a little bit of free advice scribbled in the margin. The note said the fragments were too confusing and didn't give a clear idea of the story or whether the author could write or not. The next time the writer submitted two chapters (the first and the seventh), she was asked for more details. She eventually made the sale.

Remember that you don't want to give everything away to the potential editor. You want to get her hooked enough to make her want to know more about your characters and the story. It's a careful balancing act that takes some doing but if done well, it sells the book.

And speaking of characters, if you are going to meet the challenge of writing fiction head on, you must make your characters believable. Most fiction, other than perhaps science fiction, follows life pretty closely. In other words, your plot can't be palpably false.

Obviously fiction is what it is and you can't bluff your way into the editor's heart like you might be able to do with non-fiction. Either it's a good story and well written or it's not. The editor knows from the two sample chapters and the plot summary if she is interested in considering more of what you have to say.

COMPETITION

Fiction publishers and editors are always on the lookout for the next great fantasy bestseller. These publishers will tell you that many forms of fiction follow a formula, and they would be right. For example, in romance books there is a strong and beautiful woman who is looking for "amour." She has one or more obstacles or problems to overcome that jeopardize her chances at the love she seeks. At the end of the novel she resolves the problems and finds that romance. If you don't know if your fiction book-type has a formula, find out, and find out before you do anything else.

Popcorn fiction is a term in the publishing industry that refers to fiction that isn't Pulitzer Prize material but gives the reader a good read. Science fiction, westerns and romance novels often fall into this category. Popular published authors sometimes look down on writers of popcorn fiction because it seems unworthy of any writer to produce less than award-winning literary manuscripts. However, there is a real market for these books and real money (albeit moderate) to be made in terms of volume sales.

Children's Books

If your desire is to write children's books, the procedure for submission is basically the same as it is for other types of non-fiction or how-to books. You can write a query letter, prepare a book proposal or send in the completed manuscript.

For the proposal, the parts submitted are the same as those for a non-fiction book and include a cover letter, title page, summary, specifications, market analysis, promotion, competition, author's bio and an outline, or two chapters, or the very short manuscript.

If you haven't already, take the time to browse the bookstores and libraries to see what kind of books are popular with kids today. Shelves filled with multiple books on a particular topic may be an indication you could sell one more, or show you that the market is saturated for that particular idea. Never stop browsing because the books change constantly and if you're astute, you can discover what's not there that should be.

As children's books are generally shorter than books for adults, sending in the entire manuscript might be the easiest route. If the book is for teenagers or older kids, something like the Nancy Drew series, then a proposal is called for. If the book consists of ten illustrated pages, your query letter or completed manuscript works best.

A word of caution: pay close attention to the age group for which you are writing. Just as publishing houses have specific types of books they publish, so do children's book publishers. They may focus only on a specific age group or at least have separate divisions working on publications directed at certain stages of a child's life. Some publishers may focus on either boys or girls books. These are all-important details when planning your submission.

People and particularly parents these days have an obsession with books, especially for their children, and rightly so. Reading is one way to forge an almost indestructible bond between mom, dad and kids. Books open up a new universe to children each time they pick one up. The point? As long as there are parents and kids, there are books sold. Your job is to find a book that both of them love to buy from the day the child is born to the day he or she moves out of the house.

To make good connections in the children's book industry as an author, use the same resources as mentioned in this book for adult book publishers. Most of these reference works, such as *Writer's Market*, include sources specific to children's publishing. In the library are books specifically directed at those who want to write and/or publish in this field.

It's not unheard of for novice writers hoping to break in to the children's publishing world to make great contacts at writer's conferences. Big-time editors or publishers sometimes speak at these events. They often give out business cards and ask writers to contact them if they are looking for new talent.

Don't overlook your library, book clubs, bookstores and Internet chat rooms to make contact with other writers in your genre. They are generally very supportive and will read your manuscript or offer advice if you do the same for them. They may even share their contacts with you if they feel it's deserved.

On the other hand, I know writers of children's books who are very protective of their turf and don't want to support the competition in any way. You'll simply have to find the right niche for yourself within a group that welcomes newcomers.

The reference books give the names of the editors and what they expect with a submission. Follow their guidelines. For example, the guidelines might say that, unless you plan on illustrating your children's book yourself, don't send in your amateur sketches without the editor's specific request that you do so.

Most of the time, the publisher prefers to use one of their illustrators or artists to work on a book they want to print. This doesn't mean that you can't make your ideas known. After all it's your inspiration, and you may have particular images in mind that are worth considering.

Many new authors see children's books exclusively as works of fiction. Interestingly the ratio of children's books published is forty percent non-fiction and sixty percent fiction. At my library, the kids love books like the biography of George Washington Carver — the peanut guru of the South and a son of slaves.

Anything adults want to read about so do children in a simpler more condensed version of course. There is history, nature, science and art all of which come with endless pint-sized non-fiction possibilities.

6. PROMOTION AND MARKETING

Spreading the Word

It's important to note the difference between marketing or sales and promotion as it means different things to different people. Marketing is offering a product to the public or distributors and facilitating them to buy it. Promotion is creating an awareness of a product and its availability through publicity. The two functions are different but closely intertwined because ultimately they are designed to achieve the same goal.

Due to their similarity, the functions and organization of the staffs in the two departments varies widely from publishing house to publishing house. Bigger publishing houses can have one large and well-staffed department where they carry out both functions. In a small publishing company, one or two people carry out all of the necessary promotion and marketing functions. To lift some of the burden, they may hire independent contractors on a part-time basis to help when necessary.

No matter how they are divided, sub-divided or named, the tasks are the same. They include working media of all kinds (radio, television, newspaper), placing advertising, sales to chains, clubs and individuals, foreign markets, and tours and events.

The more famous you are and the bigger the hit your publisher thinks your book is determines how much of a budget there is to promote the final product. The smaller houses simply can't do much because they don't have the money or the staff so you may have to pitch in.

89

It's possible to arrange with your publisher to share the expense or come up with a plan that you can work on jointly. For example, if you are plan on giving a lecture or doing a book signing, your publisher may arrange to have flyers and extra books available.

Well-organized promotional plans are important to peddle anything, including your book proposal. There's probably nothing you can think of that the promotion gurus of the publishing house haven't thought of or tried before. But if you come up with some decent ideas it shows you're committed to doing whatever it takes to sell the book. You might even surprise them by coming up with a unique angle.

For example, you could suggest a hook like this for a travel book: "It's not uncommon for the rich and famous to be seen vacationing or living in Belize. Francis Ford Coppola, the movie director, recently purchased a rustic but comfortable hotel on the Belizean mainland." Celebrity tidbits could do a great deal for book sales.

The key to the promotion portion of your book proposal is to emphasize your best business and promotional skills. Tell the editor how you would promote your book if it were your job to do so. Keep in mind, they probably won't use many, if any, of your ideas. Don't get hurt when they don't do what you want. These must simply be suggestions on your part. It's their role more than yours to do a good job promoting the book, but you both have a vested interest and should work together as a team.

Use all the resources you have available in all facets of your life. For example, my friend who is a personal trainer suggested in his promotional section that he would approach the gym chain he works for and ask them to sell his books at all their stores. He, in fact, already asked the management and they agreed.

Publishers won't readily want to part with their money to promote your book. This is especially true of the smaller houses. Some feel that promotion is, for the most part, a waste of time — particularly for non-fiction. They feel that the book sells itself off the shelf at the bookstore.

The logic is, if a person goes to the book outlet, he is looking for a book to buy. If yours catches his eye, he'll buy it. But I feel that if it doesn't cost me much (if anything) to promote my own book, then I should do so.

Marketing, according to those in marketing, wags the dog. According to editors however, the editors are the brains of the entire machine. There has always been a struggle of power between the two factions — try not to get caught in the middle and stick to the writing and editing side as much as you can.

Possible Resources

There are millions of subscribers to cable televisions with no shortage of viewers for the future. If you think there is a possibility of a short feature on your subject with you as a host or guest suggest it. Your appearance could include a brief book promo, which would do wonders for sales.

For example, if your book idea is on an animal species, you could pursue something on the TV show "Animal Planet." If the publisher handles wildlife books exclusively, they may be able to pull off a series or an ad promoting all their books including yours.

The same kind of possibility holds true if your book is a travel book. Try approaching the Travel Channel and see if they have any need for a host, a filler or a full-blown show on your destination.

Approach your local television station and offer to come on as a guest on any of their programs. The program directors are always looking for interesting people to interview. The length of the appearance can be a quick spot as part of a news-brief or a support role on the general topic of your book. It could also be a segment unto itself if you think you can pull it off. The point is, of course, to explain to the potential publisher what you have in mind in the promotion section of your proposal.

Free Publicity

Making potential readers aware of your intriguing book is half the sales battle. I'm sure you've heard the saying "There's no such thing as bad publicity." The more exposure, logically, the more sales. This doesn't mean you should go streaking naked across the field at Wimbledon to create stir about your tennis book!

However, if you have a friend who owns a hot air balloon, ask him to let you distribute 1,000 flyers from the air over a fair or shopping center. Design the flyer yourself on your computer. Then go to a local print shop where it's relatively inexpensive to have copies made. Think outside the box.

Be sure of course, to clear your hot air balloon antics with the people on the ground who are left to clean up the mess. And also cover yourself by checking with your local government officials to see if you need a permit or license.

If your local community or city has fairs or shows of any kind, see if you can get them to give you a booth where you can set up your books and give a presentation. If you have slides or a video, try to run them there. At the very least, approach the organizers and see if you can distribute flyers.

Who You Know

Tell the editors whom you know and be a namedropper. For example, for my Belize book proposal I wrote, "Having lived in Belize for ten years, I am a personal friend of the Director of The Belize Tourist Board. He is willing to help promote this guide-book as he travels all over the US and the world telling people about his jewel in the Caribbean."

I also mentioned that I am a close friend of the owner of the only travel agency on Ambergris Caye — the largest island off the coast of Belize and a huge tourist draw. While selling tours, she is willing to promote my book.

Take a moment to write a list of all the people you know who can play a role in your publicity campaign. Call them up or send them a note asking for ideas that are fun and beneficial to both of you.

Approach the people who share a membership with you in a writers group or club. As everyone is there for the same purpose and with the same interests, perhaps as a group you could organize a book fair. The size and informality of the group doesn't make any difference to the outcome if it's well organized and publicized.

The object is to create interest in your subject by getting close to any group of people you know that shares any interest in the subject of your book. For example, if you've written a book on guitars, pass out flyers at the next meeting you attend for your Alma Mater or the college campus where you took guitar lessons last summer.

I have a cousin living in Maine belongs to an organization that sews costumes for the largest theatre company in the region. If your book were about Shakespeare and his life on the stage, this would be a great outlet for selling books. Consider all possible associations and angles.

Radio

Radio talk shows are the hot thing these days. If you know of any shows where an appearance from you would add interest, say so to the publisher in your promotion section.

Approach the program director and see if he or she would allow you some airtime to promote a book and to entertain the listeners. You may be invited and you may not but it's worth a try, and if you are summoned, it looks good on your bio.

With radio, you may find you're welcome to fill some of their program time but it may be during the wee hours of the night or morning. You may think this isn't worth it, but again, there is no such thing as bad publicity. You never know who is watching or listening. Someone may pick up the show and want you to appear on their program too; stranger things have happened.

Getting an ad on the radio for you and/or your book is something most people would consider too expensive and they would probably be right. However, if you and your book are going to make a big splash, the publishing house may be willing to spring for ads that air across the nation or locally to coincide with a tour or speaking engagement.

Book Signings and Tours

Books signing tours are something every author dreams of. Sorry to disappoint you, but it's unlikely you warrant this kind of lavish treatment from the publisher unless you are a well-known author. Perhaps you will be one day. In the meantime, try to set up book signings in your local area. The publisher may support your endeavors by helping with flyers or extra copies of the book.

Try book signings in bookstores, malls, travel agencies and group meetings if the topic of your book is appropriate for those places. For example, if you wrote a cookbook on Christmas cookies, see if you can use the season to your advantage. Talk to someone at the Target store in your neighborhood and get a table set up with samples of the cookies and the book.

These days book signings are becoming more and more common and as a sad result attendance can be disappointing. There are a couple of tactics you can try so as not to feel completely humiliated if this happens.

Check frequently to make sure the bookstore manager or PR person puts up posters, informs the local media and promotes your coming at least two weeks before the actual event. If they don't, you are sure to have a dismal failure on your hands.

Try pairing up with another author who has a similar or completely contrary book topic to yours. At least you'll have someone to chat with and the two of you together may entice people as opposed to a lone person sitting at a desk or table.

Take items with you that draw interest. For example, when I'm doing a signing for my *Kenya Guide* book, I take African artifacts that I know people want to touch and ask questions about. Perhaps you could also try a slide show that contains pictures showing you climbing that rock wall or visiting that country or doing whatever it is you've written about. Play some music relevant to your topic if you can. All these things draw people in and maybe they'll buy your book.

One cookbook author I know takes samples of baked goods and other tasty treats for the patrons to try. Another option is to take a TV and VCR that runs a continual loop of an interview or book review that you've done in the past. This lends credibility and interests to you and your book.

Don't overlook the option of a virtual book signing. There are marketing companies that do nothing but set up virtual book tours or chats online. The expenses associated with these tours can be relatively high for authors who don't have much money but they are cheaper than traveling around the country. If you don't want to spend any money, then you can set up the publicity yourself by getting booked on smaller chat rooms. Take a look at the book club or chat section of all the major sites.

Publishers allow their authors to buy books at a discounted rate, which is usually forty percent off the list price. This can be great if you are able to do any promotions on your own and sell your own books. Obviously the percentage of profit for you goes up from the x percent royalty you've agreed to. The reduced price of the books can sometimes be negotiated into your contract or it may be stated there as part of the publisher's standard contract.

If the publishing house you're working with is large enough to offer you a book tour, that's great. You will probably stay at friends' houses and feel embarrassed when three people show up at the bookstore. But consider yourself lucky to be touring, no matter how many fans show up.

In order for a medium-sized to large publishing house to consider putting you on tour, the staff must first be convinced you can handle the job. This is where your bio is a great help to them. If you say you have stage fright and have never spoken in front of a crowd, there goes your tour. They need to be sure you won't turn out to be an embarrassment. If, however, you say you've lectured and spoken to groups of fifty or more, there's a chance you might be chosen to tour. If you are on tour for a house, you represent the publisher as well as yourself.

Magazine Advertising

Magazine advertising is often an expensive proposition but it may not be out of the question if you can convince your publisher it has an impact on book sales. They may be willing to place the ad in an appropriate and relevant magazine venue either as a full-blown ad or a three-line mention in the listing section. For example, if your book is about cats and their care, an ad in *Cat Life* magazine could well draw buyers.

Another approach may be to write an article for a magazine whose subject is related to the topic of your book. In exchange for the article and hopefully a small check, you may be able to barter for a promotional ad, a byline mentioning your book, or at least a link to your website. If the magazine isn't interested in an article, perhaps you can offer them an excerpt from your book with the same trade in mind. Say, for example, that you write a travel article on a particular destination the magazine is about to cover. There may be a good argument for placing an advertisement for the book. It is good for the magazine's readers and good for you.

If your publisher isn't interested in helping with the costs of an ad and you can't find a magazine that's willing to barter copy for an ad, consider purchasing classified advertising. This is a relatively inexpensive form of marketing that can bring in significant returns.

Some magazines may be willing to negotiate a deal with you in one of several ways. For example, they may receive all the orders that come in for your book and process them for you at ten percent cost to you per order. Another option may be for the magazine to share the revenues with you for every book order placed. In other words, a percentage of every book order automatically reverts to the magazine. This arrangement can be great as it avoids having to come up with cash up-front. The downside for the magazine, of course, is if no book orders come in.

Conventions and Exhibits

Book publishers have trade conventions and exhibits just like most industries. Each year there are hundreds of trade shows or fairs all across the country for swimming pool and hot tub manufacturers. At these shows, the new lines and updated products are put on display for installers, builders and retailers to see what's new and to place orders for the coming year.

Year after year, the same people show up for these regional, national and international conventions. The location varies a little from time to time but for the most part the organizers keep the same venues and dates to facilitate the attendees planning their annual schedules.

For each industry, there is usually one to three large shows that are the main focus each year. Everyone attends these biggest conventions and also their own local shows. Many businesses however, only send a representative or two at the most to the smaller shows. Everything depends on the size of the staff and the budget available to determine how many staff members attend and to which shows.

The same sort of exhibit is arranged for book publishers and editors. For the most part, the attendees are industry personnel who already know each other. The public can usually get in for a fee (as do the attendees) which can vary from show to show.

There are several websites that have all kinds of information for state, city, and country show listings. They have links to the "show" hotels with special rates for attendees. You can often find coupons, exhibitor lists, maps and contact information.

A great place to find these fairs is through a book entitled *Book Fairs: An Exhibiting Guide for Publishers*. It's produced by Para Publishing (www.ParaPublishing.com), or you can get it through *Publisher's Weekly* (212- 463-6758, www.publishersweekly.com).

I've found that if the show is exclusively for industry insiders, I can often present a business card and wangle my way in. The people collecting, distributing and tracking the ticket sales are hired by the show organizers and actually work for an independent company not affiliated to anyone in the industry or are part of the staff at the convention center itself. They don't offer too much resistance.

It's also possible to register online ahead of time. If you buy your entry ticket up front you can get significant savings. Depending on the size of the show and how far ahead you register, savings can be anywhere from twenty dollars to two-hundred dollars.

Inside the show, the publishing house or distributor rents a booth or table and sets up their book wares. If you can attend, it's a great place to meet editors, get to know the players in the industry and see what titles are exhibited. The competition between exhibitors can be friendly or cutthroat.

There are a few standard unspoken "rules" of etiquette that most attendees follow. For example, if you're privileged enough to meet an editor or publisher, don't give him your manuscript. He won't want to see it and certainly won't lug it home in his suitcase.

These shows are a place to mingle, see what is on display and make contacts, not a place to do any hard selling unless you're asked to do so. Friendly banter and handshakes does more for you at this point than anything else. Get names and collect business cards for later follow-up. You might gently mention your book idea and see what kind of reaction you get. If the reaction is negative, be graceful about accepting it and move on.

Clubs, Associations, Seminars and Speeches

The hard part of getting on the speaking rosters for clubs and associations is just that, getting on their list. Once you have established yourself and proven that you can entertain the guests or members and that you actually show up, the good word on you spreads. One good source on the web for finding speaking engagements is www.shawguides.com.

For the beginner, one option is volunteering at nursing homes, the local Chamber of Commerce, The Rotary Club and any other clubs or organizations with a community based focus. They are always looking for guests to participate in their monthly meetings.

Try approaching the school system or an instructor that teaches the subject you wrote about. They often have "substitute teachers" come in to make their classes fun or to help cover a particular topic in the curriculum. Start by speaking to the administration and work your way directly to the teacher.

Speaking engagements at travel clubs and tour groups about your experiences and your book would be a great promotion. Make note that these events travel around the country at different times of year and are usually at the same place and same time. Put it on your calendar and contact the event planners this year for next year.

The list of book clubs is endless and each one is designed to cater specifically to the readers of a particular genre and can be found on the Internet or in the library. For example, there is the Military Book Club, The Movie/Entertainment Book Club, History Book Club, Art Book Society, Evangelical Book Club, Ecological Book Club, Cookery Book Club, How-to Book Club, Technical Book Club, Garden Book Club, and the list goes on. If your book falls into one of these categories, try getting your book on their list or get invited to participate with the group.

More difficult to get into are the ever-popular Book-of-the-Month Club and Reader's Digest Book Clubs. These, of course, appeal to a more general audience and offer a much wider selection of topics. Nonetheless, these types of clubs also offer a tremendous potential audience if you can get yourself into their ranks.

Whenever you get the chance to avail yourself of any opportunities like these, do so, and don't forget to put out flyers when you get there. You may only make one book sale, but one is better than none and you never know where it will lead.

Websites and the Internet

For not too much money, these days you can have a professional looking website of your own. If you are a first-time author, it's probably best to have the site set up to promote your book and not you. In other words, you don't want to have photos of your last family reunion and your diary posted. Obviously, it looks unprofessional.

If you're interested in promoting yourself as a speaker, writer, lecturer or teacher, your website may be helpful to anyone in need of that kind of talent. Carefully craft a visually pleasing web page detailing what you have done, what you are available to do, how much you charge (if anything) and how someone can get in touch with you.

It's perfectly acceptable to post writing clips of your work for anyone to review, biographical information, and when you are appearing next and for what. Encourage communication with guests via e-mail and offer a "Comments" page or visitor's log.

Keeping up a website may not be something you are familiar with. It isn't too difficult with all the self-help and cheat-sheets available through your Internet provider. These companies usually offer a free template of a certain size and you just fill in the copy and photographs.

Hypertext Markup Language (HTML) is the language used on the web. It isn't hard to learn and execute if you have time. There are even online tutorials that walk you through the steps.

There are always classes being given at the local community college which are a great way to get started but can be more complicated that they're worth if you aren't interested in getting too deeply involved. Go for the beginners class and attend with determination to learn and keep it up.

If you aren't interested in doing it yourself, for a relatively small fee (either monthly or by the hour) you can find a webmaster to maintain and change your site as you direct. If the price is too steep for your budget, approach that same community college or local university to find the professor or teacher of the Internet/web subjects and ask them to recommend a budding techie to help you.

There is nothing wrong with having links to the booksellers that carry your book — in fact I would encourage it. This way, if someone finds your book and/or your site they can easily and quickly purchase the publication online through a link to a reputable store.

If you can find professionals to endorse your book and/or you as a writer, you may want to have links to their websites too. The more people that say you and your book are great, the more people believe it and the more books you'll sell.

Take the time to do a web search on the subject you are covering in your book and see if there are any sites out there that you think are worth linking to. Once you've found them, ask permission for a reciprocal link and do so.

For example, if your book is about alternative methods of pain management, find legitimate acupuncturists or their association (if they have one) who would be willing to have a link to your site in exchange for a link to theirs.

Every thirty to forty days, it's a good idea to submit your Uniform Resource Locator (URL) and the key words regarding your book to the search engines that accept free submissions. This way, anyone searching for your Cajun cookbook finds it. From all over the world and the country people are quickly, and at no cost to you, sent to your site. This is a fabulous deal.

If you can manage a website but you don't have a scanner or the tools to get photographs or a copy of the cover of your book onto a disk you can ask your publisher if he has a copy he can e-mail to you. If this isn't an option, take the cover or photos to the local print shop. They can scan the images you need onto a disk for a nominal fee.

Managing a simple website is the most basic of marketing venues for an author, but to promote, sell and build web traffic over the Internet and be very successful at it takes a whole new, difficult and time consuming set of skills. For myself, as an author, I want to write, and don't feel like I have the time to maintain a site. Besides, marketing isn't my forte. But can I afford not to promote my work? No. If it's not promoted and no one knows about it then obviously it won't sell.

If you decide you want someone to manage your book's promotion and marketing over the Internet, there are companies available to do just that. For a setup fee of anywhere from $300 to $8,000 and a reasonable monthly maintenance fee of $50.00 a month you can have someone do the work for you. Two sites to take a look at are www.bookzone.com and www.authorsontheweb.com.

There are so many options for using the Internet to promote yourself and your book online in addition to the few I mention here. One source of guidance is a great little book titled, How to Publish and Promote Online (St. Martin's Press), www.stmartins.com. It includes dozens of ways and places to support your book online. Some for a fee and others free except for the hard work you'll have to put in.

There are many other web promotional options worth looking into. Start an e-magazine or e-zine of your own. Compile a mailing list and send out a monthly or weekly e-mail newsletter. Constantly change the content of your website with articles and excerpts. Think about strategic alliances or sponsors. Target information to a subject-specific newsgroup or program director. And, post audio clips online of you reading from your book.

The Internet and web possibilities are endless. It's a disservice to yourself if you don't use the resource. You put too much effort into your book to let it sit without pushing it where you can.

Mailings

Take a trip to your local post office and ask to speak to the Postmaster. He is the most knowledgeable person there and should know the best and cheapest way to go about doing a mailer. The clerks may also know and you can try them, but in my experience, they are generally too disinterested to bother with.

What I would suggest is either a postcard or a folded 8-1/2 inches by 11 inches flyer. For approximately thirty-one cents per piece, the post office folds and distributes the flyer to any zip code you desire. That's a relatively cheap rate to get your book exposure in a specific area. For example, for my book on Kenya I selected a local, suburban wealthy part of town and sent postcards to that zip code.

In my post card I offered to help them with their safari planning and suggested we meet whenever it was convenient for them. I had a presentation prepared along with photos, slides and Kenyan artifacts. I met with the interested people who, at the very least, bought a book from me and sometimes wanted to take the next step and go to Kenya.

I then teamed up with a safari planner who agreed to make all the bookings and take the safari with the clients. The promotion was a success for the travelers, as they felt safe being guided through the ins and outs of travel to and from Kenya. I sold books, so I was happy, and the safari planner came out on top too. Later I went on safari and saw other tourists with my book — what a great feeling!

The Postmaster may have other ideas about how to get your postcard or flyer out more cheaply or to a wider audience. Things change and the post office sometimes has promotions or new programs. Take the time to visit them.

Newspapers

The newspapers in your area are usually willing to support local talent. Try to get to know the editors and feel them out for ideas on how the two of you can work together on getting you, your book and its subject into their publications. You might ask them to lunch and see what suggestions they come up with. Newspaper folks don't make much money, so offering to buy lunch in exchange for picking their brains for ideas might be worth the investment. If nothing else, you'll make a new friend.

There is a listing in most weekend papers citing the location, phone number and time of interesting local events. This is free in most papers and is a great place to get your book event promoted for absolutely nothing. Make sure you call them up with plenty of notice, as the lead-time is several weeks ahead of the print and distribution date.

If you think you might warrant a full-blown article on yourself as a local character of interest, contact the newspapers in your area and suggest a feature article. For example, the editors at *The Atlanta Journal and Constitution* were kind enough to do several great articles as I tried to push sales for *Kenya Guide*. Over the course of several months, they wrote a couple of articles about me as the author. Then they asked me to write some travel articles on Kenya and in addition we did a few question and answer pieces also on Kenya. The book sales didn't rocket off the charts, but they did go up, and, it was fun.

At the bookstore in your neighborhood or library, take a look at those that have a review column. Call or e-mail the editor and see if they would be willing to do a review of your book. Even if you simply get a short paragraph, the exposure is worth the effort. Sometimes, if your publisher thinks the book warrants it, he'll send a free copy to the *New York Times* or other noteworthy newspapers and book reviewers.

E-mail

Consider e-mail your best friend and your least successful promotional opportunity. On the one hand, because of the enormous amount of unwanted e-mail (SPAM) that gets sent around the world (and the possibility e-mail carries a deadly virus), most of us simply delete anything in the mailbox from an unknown source. On the other hand, everyone uses e-mail as a matter of course when conducting business.

Apart from anything else, e-mail is the fastest and most affordable way to communicate. Attaching a scanned-in writing sample, a promotional flyer or a Word document containing a book proposal is easier than falling out of bed.

There is, however, some debate as to how attachments are perceived. Some business people say they won't open any attachments unless they asked for and are expecting them. Others are fine with receiving unsolicited attachments. For what you want to do as far as your publicity efforts, it may be best to call and ask permission or check the company's website for guidelines on what preferences they have.

The key here, of course, is to use e-mail wisely and as effectively as possible. For example, if you are promoting yourself as a speaker, teacher or author to radio stations or booksellers, say so in your subject line and address the e-mail using the correct name of the program or publicity manager. You're more likely to get a response if you're e-mail is directed to someone specific and if the subject line is very clear about what is enclosed.

Don't ever use too light or very dark background color on your screen. First of all, it makes reading the copy difficult when the colors conflict or create glare. Second of all, it looks unprofessional unless you are a graphic artist and that's the whole point.

E-mail is so easy to use that we sometimes tend to forget that what we put in it must be carefully crafted and professionally written. What I'm saying is, use your spellchecker and don't just dash off an e-mail because you get a half-baked idea. You're unlikely to get a response, and if you do, it is probably not what you want to hear.

If you have any doubt about the recipient's ability to open whatever you attach, then it would be best to paste it into the body of the e-mail rather than attach it. Protocol for this sort of situation in today's business world often dictates that whatever is in the attachment be pasted into the body of the e-mail in ASCII or plain text format. The rules also call for all formatting to be removed including "smart quotes," special characters and graphics.

This e-mail tool is particularly effective if you want to get in touch with overseas agents, editors, publishers or promoters. It saves a bundle both in terms of money and time. Again, be specific in your subject line and it may help avoid the delete key.

An e-mail press release or publicity notice for your book is a great way to get bookstores, club and other interested groups to notice you. For a long press release write no more than 300 words and for a short one 100 words is good. Be sure to include who you are, what your book is about, what you can do for them and contact information.

If you choose to start your own e-newsletter or e-zine, make sure the format is easy and simple to read. Find a mailing list on the web (www.listz.com or www.egroups.com) and see what's required to use them. But most of all, be prompt with your delivery each month or quarter and keep the contents fresh.

Don't forget to use an e-mail signature, which is a superbly subtle way of marketing. What is it? It's a few lines of text that automatically attaches to the end of your e-mail each time you send one. It should be no longer than six lines and include a URL for your website. It can promote you, your book, a sale, a book signing event or anything else you want readers to see. According to some experts, this simple tag line can increase hits to your website or book orders by seventy-five percent!

Giveaways and Logos

When I need a pen or a marker for the book I'm using for research I dig around in a drawer full of such things. The items I end up selecting are often those I receive as a promotion from the bank, my insurance agent or the cruise I went on last summer. They have memories and familiar faces attached to them and I like to remember the connections. I appreciate the effort they made to send me the knick-knack. Sometimes I select the pen or pencil based simply on the bright color. I know I'm not the only one.

Giveaways can make the difference between your being remembered or forgotten along with the hundreds of others who seek publicity, are out to impress a new editor or are trying to market themselves and their upcoming book.

Start out small by ordering under a hundred items. Choose things that people use year round. Some of the most sought after items are calendars, pens, pencils, wallet calendars, bookmarks, mousepads or key chains.

The extra bit of attention to an editor, club or bookseller gets you noticed and may even make the difference between success and failure. Remember, however, to either address the item to a specific person or send more than one. If you don't use a particular name and/or send only one, there's no telling where the item ends up (in the employee kitchen) or with whom it goes home.

Another way to separate yourself from the crowd and make a statement is with your letterhead, business cards and envelopes.

Most writers simply use run-of-the-mill manila envelopes or plain white number tens. How about your own classy logo and professionally printed items?

Your logo, for example, can be a source of free promotion if you make it memorable. If you know someone who is an artist or designer, ask him or her to help you. Begin by looking at your local library for books on design, graphics and type. Find some samples of things that catch your eye and offer these as a starting point to the designer.

Some people like to use their initials. Others use a design, and some, a humorous or memorable motto or phrase. I'd suggest selecting a couple of type faces, type sizes, symbols, borders, drawings and any samples you think you'd like. If they don't have a clue what you like, it makes their job a lot harder and may end up wasting a lot of time. Whatever it is it must be striking.

If you don't know anyone who can inexpensively design something for you and you can't do it yourself, try going to a graphic arts school or local college. Ask for the department head and see if she would be willing to let the class or a student design your logo as a project. If not, let her recommend a star pupil to do it as a freelance project for a nominal fee.

These days, with electronic layout programs, the design is relatively simple to produce electronically and any print shop can use a diskette to run business cards, letterhead, envelopes, or other items for you. For your reference, here are some places to look for more information on promotional items:

1Stop Promotional Products, http://store.yahoo.com/1stopshop

GoPromos.com

Instant Promotion.com

www.logo-motion.com

CPI Line, www.promobooks.com/dealers.htm

Iprint, www.iprint.com

7. THE FINAL TWO PARTS

The Author's Bio

When you're preparing your bio, take into account the two categories into which your experience is likely to fall. First there are your writing credentials if you have any, and second there are your credentials as an expert in the field you're writing about. Think of any testimonials you have in terms of these two headings and categorize them accordingly.

Let the publisher get to know you. If you propose a book on organization in the home, explain that you spent your Thanksgiving Day doing what you love to do best — reorganizing and alphabetizing the spices in your sister's kitchen cabinets. This will probably get a chuckle and show you are the right person to write this book.

If, by chance, you're proposing a book on scuba diving in the top three most acclaimed dive spots, it's important to mention you grew up living in a shack on the beach off Australia's Great Barrier Reef. Describe what you saw as you went for your daily dive. Not only are you interesting and unique, but it makes the book far more saleable because of your angle.

Education might be of interest to the publisher if it makes you more credible or accomplished. If, for example, you stuck with the academics and pursued your Masters and Ph.D. in veterinary medicine, you clearly should be the one to write a book on training and keeping your cat healthy in his senior years.

Being educated and getting good grades gives insight into the kind of commitments that you are willing to make and how you'll meet them. Mentioning these things could give you the edge

107

over another potential book proposal on the publisher's desk. If you dropped out of college after two years and were only getting passing grades, it might not be a good idea to say so unless you're proposing a book on how to succeed in life (and what jobs pay best) without a college degree.

If you're a book author, it's a grave error not to add it to your biography. A book or two with your name on the cover definitely catches a publisher's attention and indicates your ability to present and produce a publishable book.

Any other publications you were involved in, either as the writer, editor or copy editor, are worth mentioning also. It doesn't matter if the work is a brochure pamphlet or technical manual, as long as you can show you were part of the publishing process.

If the number of publications you've worked on is impressive, include it. Also include the titles (newspapers or magazines) if they are well known and lend prestige to your cause.

If you have anything that's published, even if the topic doesn't relate to your book proposal, mention it. I had many articles published in many magazines and newspapers across the country, which certainly helped with my first proposal. If someone thinks you are worthy of being published, that's one step closer to giving you some credibility as a writer and getting your book accepted.

I'd venture to guess that most publishers would take your word for it that you have writing samples if you say so. It wouldn't be worth the risk to lie. I didn't send along any samples or copies of my published materials as part of the proposal package but I said they were available if anyone wanted to see them. You can do the same.

Distinctions of any kind that lend credibility to you as a person or to you as an expert must find a spot on you bio. Perhaps you have published reviews about your work. If so, include snippets and quotes from them in your bio. Be sure to mention the original in its entirety is available upon request.

Maybe you were invited to be a guest speaker on several occasions or have a membership to an impressive organization. Disclose it if you think it helps the editor decide your book proposal is worth more serious consideration because of what you bring to the process.

The author's biography can be as long or as short as you see fit to make it providing the credentials are pertinent to the book you're trying to sell. In general however, I'd suggest keeping the sketch of you on the shorter rather than the longer side.

The task of selling yourself as a potential author won't be easy, especially if you don't have previously published books. It wasn't for me. I re-wrote my proposal bio at least six times.

For my travel book, for example, I wrote anything I could think of in my life that was remotely related to traveling and being international. You must do the same with anything in your life that's associated to the subject matter of your proposed book.

It gets less difficult to write your bio with each passing book you publish. Once I sold my first book, the task of preparing a proposal and the bio that goes with it was easier. Then, my second book came out and I felt I proved myself to prospective publishers. They saw that I was up to the task and assumed I had the discipline and knowledge to give them something we could sell.

The Outline, Table of Contents and Chapters

Let's suppose you researched your subject and gathered enough material to convince you and anyone who will listen, that this is a meaty, valuable non-fiction book. Now, it's time to gather all your notes and jot your thoughts and ideas down in an organized fashion.

Before you try to break down the non-fiction book by chapters, arrange the information you have into a logical progression of ideas. Think of it as teaching someone how to do something and put each step of the lesson in sequential order. Jot, jot and jot using quick phrases and short sentences. When this is done, break your list into "chunks" of related and flowing ideas. Compile each of these sections under a major heading, which in turn becomes a chapter title. This is your outline.

At the end of the task, this outline easily becomes the table of contents (or "TOC" in publishing lingo). Your TOC soon becomes your chapters and then quickly morphs into the substance of the manuscript.

Your outline is essential to avoid getting confused once the book gets to over 100 pages. It's impossible to keep up with what you've said and where, without referring back to the outline/ TOC. If you don't do one, you'll keep repeating yourself and waste time wondering if you've included this or that already.

Choose at least nine main subjects or topics to become chapter headings. If you have more than nine, that's fine. All it means is your book has more chapters. For each chapter heading, there should be at least five sub-headings under which any relevant information fits. Keep breaking your outline down into smaller and smaller sections under sub-headings until everything you've collected fits somewhere. This work is very valuable and definitely worth doing well. Consider this the building of your foundation. Build a weak foundation and your house crumbles.

In the outline you submit to the publishing house, you may not want to include every little detail you've jotted down. It's probably too much information, when all they want to see is the bigger picture. They don't particularly want to read an outline including each paragraph topic. Instead, take a look at the lists you've made and pick out between five and eight of the most interesting and important facts for each chapter. To make the chapters in the non-fiction proposal more visually appealing, you may chose to use bullets or symbols to separate each thought. That's up to you, but whatever you do, keep it simple.

Some writers like to use index cards for their ideas. This way they can move them around, depending in which chapter they best belong. I prefer to use Word on my computer to keep up with my outline/Chapters/TOC. I easily move the information around when I think it fits better under a different heading. I keep a printed copy next to me as a quick reference when I begin the actual writing process.

Your outline is not written in stone. It's certainly easier for you once you begin writing not to have to change much, but to simply flesh it out. If it does change a little, it doesn't create much of a stir with the editor. Editors and publishers realize your outline is a guide to sell your idea and to introduce them to the meat of the book. As you start writing, you may find that something needs to be added or re-arranged. Do it without fear of consequence.

Of course, this doesn't mean that if you sold a book on drag racing and suddenly decided you wanted to write a book on roses instead that you should. If you did, you'd never expect to get your book into print or to write for that publishing house again.

A Word Regarding the Index

The index pages are the last pages of the book and in my opinion are invaluable for quick reference. Here, each time a word or phrase is mentioned in the manuscript it appears in the index with the corresponding page number. For example, in the index of this book you can look up each time a reference is made to the word catalog.

Some books don't have an index, which is a disservice to the reader. I won't buy a non-fiction book that does not have an index, nor will most people. The index is critical to non-fiction because people often refer to the book again and again when they want to be reminded of a fact or look up a detail they have forgotten. It's well known that books without indexes don't sell as well as those with indexes.

Who prepares the index varies from publishing house to publishing house. But it's important for you to find out whose task it is, if for no other reason than it very time consuming. First check your contract as it's often stated there if it is the author's responsibility.

You may think you have completed your end of the bargain and are ready to move on to the next writing assignment only to discover that the manuscript is on your doorstep ready for indexing!

Some writing programs available to authors have an automatic indexing tool available as part of the software. To create an index, mark the index entries — which can be words, phrases or symbols — in your document. Once these are marked, you can choose an index design and build the finished index. The software program collects the marked words, sorts them alphabetically, references the page numbers and removes any duplicate entries.

If you prepare the index on your manuscript, it won't be valid any longer once the edits, re-writes and reformatting are done at the publisher. The indexing program must be run again using the new manuscript and in the correct format.

In the larger houses, there is a department designed to handle this large and important chore. The staff may enter the indexing codes using a software program as they prepare the manuscript and while it is being edited. Once editing is complete, the indexing program quickly performs its function electronically.

At other times, a hard copy of the manuscript is returned to the author once all copy changes have been made in order for the index to be produced manually. At this stage all the page numbers are where they will be in the final printed copy so it's a relatively easy but time consuming task to read each page, pull out the key words and annotate them.

If the indexing task should fall to you but you decide you don't have time or the patience to follow-through, consider a professional indexer. To find such people, check the websites or library references for Literary Market Place, Editorial Freelancers Association or EEI.

About the Cover

The cover, any book publisher will tell you, is the most critical part of a book. You want your cover to sell the publication for you. It should jump off the shelf at the potential reader and make them buy it over and above all the other books displayed.

I think it's safe to say that the simpler and more understated your cover image is, the stronger that idea presents itself. For example, if your book is about wealth building, a stack of 100-dollar bills or a gold bar will convey the message clearly and provide support for the title. A great cover always ties the graphic elements and the title together.

Covers can be very expensive to produce and anything in color is considerably more expensive to run on a press than black and white. So, right off the bat, if you are going to have a color cover, and most books do, the expenses are mounting. Keep in mind, however, that more often than not, the spine of the book is what the buyer actually sees first on the bookseller's shelf. That makes your design, color usage and title critical.

If you are like most people, you let your eyes skim along the spines of the books with your head cocked sideways. On the spine, the design and colors are the first thing to jump out at you followed, closely by the title. When this happens, you'll pull the book out, skim through it, and make your decision to buy or not.

Deciding if the book should have a soft (paperback) or hardcover depends on what kind of book it is and who will buy it. For example, if it's a coffee table book full of high-gloss color photographs of all the different body styles of Corvette to ever run off the assembly line, naturally, you expect it to be expensive and have a hardback cover.

If, on the other hand, it's a book about the irrefutable facts of pouring concrete back-yard pads, you might expect it to be a paperback with few if any color photographs and maybe some illustrations.

If the decision is that the book is a paperback with color on the cover, it is less expensive to produce than a hardback book with a color cover and a jacket to match. This is why most trade publishing houses opt for paperbacks.

Another expense the publisher faces when deciding what kind of cover to put on any book is the cost of binding. If the paperback book is perfect-bound (which means it's glued together down the spine) or saddle-stitched (stapled down the spine) it's far more cost effective than a hardbound book. Most books are in fact perfect-bound because other types of bindings don't sit or stack well on shelves. To put together a hardcover book, glue is also involved and it requires much more skilled and labor intensive work.

Booklets, tracts, pamphlets and small publications are usually saddle-stitched because they cannot be perfect-bound. If a book has less than sixty-four pages, the spine, at less than 1/8 of an inch, is too small to glue. The exception here is for children's books, where a special process called **juvenile binding** is used on publications with as few as sixteen pages.

To overcome the problem of a book being too small to perfect bind, it's possible to use thicker paper to build up the size. But a higher price for the paper may not make this a feasible option depending on the size of the print run and other cost factors.

If the cover has to be designed and created by an artist or illustrator, it is expensive to produce both in terms of paying the artist and in production costs. Publishers, of course, take all these things into account when deciding if a book is cost effective to pursue.

When you are putting together your book proposal, you may be able to use the cover to your advantage as an additional tool to get the publisher to want you to write the manuscript. If you can come up with a great idea for a cover that won't cost the publisher an arm and a leg, it may give you the advantage if the editorial board is trying to choose between a couple of projects.

Show the publisher you have the perfect cover design idea by describing it in detail. Phrase your idea as a suggestion and make sure you know what you're talking about. They may hate what you offer, but on the other hand they may not. And, if they can see where they can save money, it might be a done deal.

When I became a writer, I discovered that when selling my articles, if I could provide photographs, (usually slides) I had a much greater chance of making the sale. I went out and bought a great camera and took some classes that have paid off well over the last fifteen years.

Most articles must have illustrations of some sort, and they can be expensive and troublesome to acquire from other sources. If I told the editor I had twenty slides to choose from for inside and cover material, they always wanted to see them and most of the time I made the sale. The same applies to books.

For example, when I wrote *Kenya Guide*, I had hundreds of slides available for consideration. Eventually the publisher selected a few for the back and front covers of the book and paid me a small fee. I'd like to think that it helped make the sale when I mentioned the photo availability in my book proposal.

Another option, besides taking the photographs yourself, is to find a source that you can offer the publisher. Say, for example, you're writing a book on fishing for trout in North Carolina. Get in touch with the not-for-profit organization Trout Unlimited, and see if you can "borrow" some images from them. You may have to pay a nominal fee (which the publisher may cover) or you might simply have to give the organization and/or the photographer credit.

The point is, if you come up with this workable solution, it saves the publisher a great deal of time, effort and ultimately, expense. Your endeavor is much appreciated, especially if the publishing house is a small one.

Unless it's very appropriate (for a biography of your family?) I would stay away from suggesting family snapshots or a drawing done by your child. This might be cute but the publisher probably won't think too much of it. At the very least, wait until you've signed the contract to make your recommendation.

Ultimately, it's the publisher's decision as to what goes on the cover of your book. Most of the time the author gets a chance to wade in and offer her take on what should appear. No one may listen, but at least you'll feel that you've had your say.

The Title

Choosing a title for your book can make or break the sale of your proposal. The title on the cover page tells the editor (and eventually your readers) at a glance whether the subject matter is something the publishing house is interested in. Be careful what you name your creation.

Someone once told me that when you are going on a job interview, the person doing the interviewing has made up his or her mind about you within the first thirty seconds of meeting you. It takes that little time to decide to write off a potential employee, or to keep listening.

Think of any first meeting as if it were in an elevator and the two of you were going down together. Five seconds is the approximate time it takes to reach the ground floor. In that time you must say your name and your title — which should explain clearly what you do.

If you adapt these theories to book titles, you can see how it's important to make your very best impression quickly. You want to hook the editor, keep him on the line and let him know right away what the book is about.

The title of a book sometimes comes to a writer in the most natural way with never a doubt as to what it should be. Other writers complete the proposal and sometimes the book itself before a title emerges. What I'm saying is, don't try to force a title out of your brain. Most of the time, the muse flows when the time is right.

I like to "listen" during that magical moment between being awake and falling asleep. If I have been worrying at a word, idea, title or course of action, I stop trying then and in my semiconscious state the obvious answers appear. Try it and see what happens.

A friend told me a story about Leonardo DaVinci. She said that this twilight time was also his best time to solve a puzzle. In order to be awake enough to write the answer or idea down, he held a bell in his hand and at the moment he fell asleep and the answer to his dilemma came, the bell fell out of his hand and woke him up. Then he wrote his thoughts down.

If your book is fiction, the title may be equally important as a non-fiction book, but there is much more creative license. You can bend the rules significantly. For non-fiction, the title needs to convey the book idea clearly. For example, *A Biography of Ronald Reagan* states clearly the subject. However, with fiction you can use something like *A River Runs Wide*, and it's up to the marketing and cover blurbs to get someone to buy it.

It's not illegal, and there is no copyright infringement, if two or more books have the same title. You want to make sure, however, you aren't using the name of a book that is a best seller or is world-famous. This would do a disservice to them and you and probably make some folks angry.

In this day and age of the Internet, use words in your title that leave no doubt in the recall of a search engine/browser, that it must pull your book up in the event someone searches for the topic. For example, if your book is a travel book on Argentina, use the word in the title. If the book is about tax shelters for your real estate investments, say so in the title. Then when a buyer searches the bookstores online for tax and real estate or Argentina, your titles pop up.

Keep the title short. Sweet and simple is better. Again, that web browser finds it easier to keep up with your title if it can fit it all in. Otherwise, you run the risk of having part of the title cut off during the search engine search. As a first-time author trying to get books sold, you'll need every little trick in the book to keep you on the playing field.

In the early stages of your book proposal, try the title out on your friends and family. See how they react and ask them to be honest. I personally prefer not to jinx the project and so I try not to talk about it. I don't want the Muse to go running screaming from my office never to return. But, superstition aside, it's a good idea to bounce it off your tongue and see how it sounds to you and those you trust.

If your title is awful, the proposal may not get past the editor's initial reaction to toss it into the return/reject pile. If the title works (for you and them) and the publisher buys the book, they may want to change it anyway. These folks do this for a living and have an instant gut reaction to titles that sell.

Don't be offended — just let them do their jobs. You'll sell more books with an unforgettable title if they can come up with one. A great example is the book *Talking Dirty (with the Queen of Clean)*. That certainly catches your eye. Despite the suggestive title, the book is about how to get anything clean using natural substances. I love the book and the title.

Don't try to be too cute, suggestive, or clever, unless you are absolutely positive it works without being trite and corny. If your book topic is a serious one, the title generally should be a serious one. If, however, you or your uncle Don comes up with something witty and original that clearly conveys the purpose of the book, go for it.

For a good title, stay away from the cliche words of our time such as "other" or "woman." Studies show these have been done to death and need to go away for a while to emerge sometime in the future when we've all forgotten about them. The same is true of using punctuation in the title. It's a distraction rather than an asset to what the book is about. Just tell the reader in simple, uncomplicated, unpunctuated English what to expect if they open the book and start reading. The editor appreciates your simplicity and directness.

In your search for a title, stay away from quotations as a general rule. If you use a quote as your title, make sure that the potential market, without any doubt at all, knows who said it and why. If you aren't positive this is the case, forget it.

Some publishers like to use subtitles, and that's great if that's what they want. By and large, however, in these days if instant gratification, it takes too long for the reader to read the title, take in its style/type etc., and then try to figure out what the book is about by searching for a subtitle. Now you've lost them and they've moved on to the next book on the shelf.

Subtitles aren't bad if the title shows what the book is about and the subtitle takes that explanation a step further. But if the title isn't clear and needs a subtitle to explain it, I'd shy away if I were you, especially for a first book. Keep it uncomplicated with one title that tells it all.

Ask yourself two questions: will this title catch and hold the attention of the reader? And, does the title quickly and succinctly describe the subject of the book? If the answer is yes to both, you've got it right.

Dedication

Once a publisher buys your book, and you are underway with the actual writing, keep in mind you have the option to dedicate your creation. Think of someone, human, animal or spirit, you might like to honor in the first few pages.

What I'd suggest is inserting a page right after the title page. Add the heading, "Dedication." Compose a line or two that makes you feel warm and fuzzy inside and center the copy from top to bottom and side to side on the blank page. A dedication is one or two short sentences and rarely any longer. If it is longer, it becomes an "Acknowledgement."

If you forget to do this, the publisher will more than likely give you the opportunity during the editing or typesetting phase to jot out a quick dedication. For a sample of how or what to write take a look inside your favorite author's books for inspiration.

Advertising/Catalog Copy

You will hear the term list as you progress through the publishing world. What this refers to is simply the list of books the publisher has for sale. Those books that are soon-to-be published are called the front list. Those that are already published but are still for sale and distribution are called the back list.

If you are dealing with a smaller publishing house, they may ask you to write advertising or catalog copy for your book. This comes, of course, after you have agreed to write the book and are in the contract phase of the negotiations.

At the larger publishing companies, they have copywriters or editors to help take care of this task. Sometimes, you have a great deal of input and sometimes they write it based on what you said in your proposal and you won't even see it. It all depends on whom you're working with.

If the job falls to you, you'll need to come up with approximately 150 words that best describe your book, what's in it and how wonderful it is. Some writers prefer to craft these few paragraphs from scratch. Rather than reinvent the wheel, however, take a look at the summary section in your book proposal and polish it to a higher degree of perfection, if that's possible.

Once written, this advertising text goes into a catalog the publisher puts out in order to let the booksellers and buyers know what publications are coming out in the upcoming seasons. The catalog helps the publisher and distributor promote and take orders for books that are in the works but aren't yet finalized. The catalog includes all anticipated and soon to be printed publications.

Books planned for upcoming seasons are on the drawing board for at least a year ahead in an effort to expedite the production of the catalog. The fall season usually begins in September and continues through the winter. The spring season begins in February and continues through the summer. Most publishing houses start each new list with two sales conferences each year. One held in June for the fall list and one held in December for the spring list.

The trade catalogs at most publishing houses are distributed twice a year to librarians and booksellers, but some of the larger companies produce three catalogs a year and may have additional conferences.

At this phase of the process, you may not know exactly what is going to be in your book. Say, for example, in May, you have a marvelously detailed book proposal with all the appropriate sections included and the publisher loves it. You finalize your contract negotiations and agree to write the book at the end of September. You are asked to produce the 150-word catalog copy at the beginning of October, but you have written only 5,000 words of your book. It's evolving, growing and taking on a life of its own. Don't panic, it's okay.

Everyone in the industry knows the detailed catalog copy may change a little as the masterpiece is molded and perfected in the hands of the author and the editor. The advertising copy is only a rough guide for buyers.

8. SAGE ADVICE

Finding the Publishers

There are many sources available to writers where you can find lists of publishers and their addresses for your book proposal. In these reference works, you'll find specifics for each publishing house and its divisions. The three most popular books are *Writer's Market, Writer's Digest* and *Writer's Handbook*. In each, it says which genre they are interested in, whether or not they accept unsolicited manuscripts directly from unpublished authors, from published authors only, submissions from agents only, or are simply too busy to accept anything at all.

Each year, *Writer's Market*'s new release is filled with more than 4,000 buyers for your writing. It includes 75 literary agents, 1,000 new publishing opportunities, 1,900 magazines, 1,100 book publishers, 700 contests and awards, 6,500 phone and fax numbers, 6,500 e-mail addresses and websites, plus noted specific editorial needs of the publisher or publication. And, if that isn't enough, it also includes submission guidelines, pay rates, royalties and advances.

You can purchase this reference book's new edition each year for $20.99, or you can find it at your local library. You cannot check it out and take it home, however, and that can be frustrating and time consuming.

The easiest way to get around this slight problem is to make copies of the pages you are interested in. Don't try to copy the entire book, just pick a couple of pages and for about ten cents a copy you can take home the data you need. Another option is to copy the information you need on a pad of writing paper for the ten to twenty publishers you'll submit to.

Another great option to explore when looking for publishers is the *Literary Market Place* (LMP, R. R. Bowker). It can be found in the reference section of most large libraries, university libraries, or through inter-library loan programs.

If your plan is to use an international publisher, then you might want to try the *International Literary Marketplace* (ILMP). This is a valid course of action if your book's subject lends itself more to the reading tastes of those outside the USA. Be aware that the entire process could take much longer due to the distance and expenses involved in dealing with an overseas business. Then, there are the issues of time differences, technology distinction and publishing/writing idiosyncrasies. It might not be a big deal, but it can create misunderstanding.

If your book is for academia, the *Association of American University Presses Directory* (AAUP Directory) is the best place to look for a publisher. As the name indicates, it's a directory listing university presses and their contact information.

There are many other books at the library and online that list contact information essential for finding publishers, agents, children's book publishers, graphic artists, illustrators, novel and non-fiction publishing houses and so on depending on how targeted your need is. The ones I mention are the most detailed and comprehensive.

Take the time to look in the front of the any of these reference works and find the publishing date. If the book is more than a year old, it may not be to your advantage to use it. The information is out of date and you may spend more time than it's worth spinning your wheels trying to use contacts that aren't valid any longer. Given the state of the economy and the state of many businesses in these precarious times, the publishers may be gone altogether or consolidated with others in the business.

When using any of these books, it's very important to follow the guidelines. If you are a first time author without an agent, for example, send your proposal only to the publishers who accept unsolicited work from unpublished authors without an agent.

Make sure you only send your proposal to the publishers who produce work of the type you are writing. It makes no sense to send a non-fiction book proposal on sewing to a publisher of poetry. It will take him ten seconds to toss it out.

It's not uncommon for publishing staff to move around to other departments, get promoted, receive title changes or simply move on to other jobs. Therefore, it's important to call each prospective publisher to verify the name and title of the person you are submitting to. Out of ten publishing houses I planned to send proposals to, one was out of business, and of the other nine, six had new submission editors. It shows a high level of professionalism that you took the time to find out who the new person is.

Taking the shortcut and sending the proposal to "The Editors" or the "Editorial Department" isn't a good idea. It may save you time and effort on the front end but you end up paying for the laziness when your work goes exactly where you've sent it — nowhere. Without a name on the front, no one feels responsible for handling your envelope. The mail-handlers deliver it to the lowliest assistant and there it sits for a while until it is delivered to someone's in-box where, again, it takes the lowest priority status.

While conducting your research on which editor to send the book proposal to, you might find that the publishing house has already produced a book with a similar topic. It could be to your advantage to call that publishing house and ask them which editor worked on that title and send your proposal to her. It may be that she is so familiar with the subject, she would be willing to do another book on it, as long as it is different enough to warrant the effort.

Submitting Your Proposal

Now the task of writing and proofreading your proposal is complete. You have edited it, run it through your spell-check program and printed a clean, fresh copy. The publisher or editor's name and address are clearly and correctly spelled. So what now?

Once more for good measure take the checklist and tick off one last time the fact you have included all the parts required for a successful and professional book proposal. Then check again to make sure you have included a phone number and contact information for yourself or your agent. It would be terrible if the publisher loved your book idea and then couldn't get in touch with you! Finally, re-read your cover letter to make certain it's the best letter of introduction you can write.

Manuscript Acceptance

Due to limited funds, time and resources, publishers can accept only a certain number of proposals, offer a certain number of contracts and print a certain number of books each year. In addition they have a delivery lead time they must work from and stick to.

In other words, they have to carefully plan a timeline for each book they produce. Once they buy it and the contracts are signed, they have a certain number of months in which the book is written edited, printed and distributed. This is not only going on with one book but with many and within different publishing seasons!

The buying decisions for booksellers are made at certain times of year — spring and fall. When submitting your proposal, it's important to take note of what time of year it is. Ask yourself if the publishers are too busy in their production and editing cycles right now. Or are they in their selling cycles? It's wise to wait until the time is right if you can. If they get your proposal on their desk as they look for new ideas, your odds of getting a book published goes up.

I sent in a book proposal to a publisher in August of 2002; it was accepted in late October of 2002. My deadline for delivery was February 1, 2003 and the book was due out in the summer of 2003. I felt like I hit the publisher's timeline just right. He was looking for books for the next season and I presented one he liked. In my experience, just before these seasons (July/August and October/November) is a good time to deliver a professional proposal for a catalog in the following year.

Variety of Publishers

As a general rule, publishing companies can be broken into five basic categories: Trade, Textbook, Scholarly, Reference and Mass Market. Books that are not hardbound or mass market are categorized as trade or paperback.

SAGE ADVICE

Trade book publishers are those that print what most people in the English speaking world read. If you say the word "trade" to most people they immediately think it means catering to a specific industry. That would be true in all instances except when referring to publishing. In the publishing world "trade" indicates any type of book sold to the general public.

Trade books are what we find at the large booksellers — how-to, novels and biographies to name a few. The trade and paper-back books come in standard sizes: 8-1/2 inches by 9 inches, 6 inches by 9 inches, the most common 5-1/2 inches by 8-1/2 inches, and 8-1/2 inches by 11 inches.

Textbook publishers print textbooks for schools, colleges and universities. When you were in school, you were given a list of books you'd need to buy for the year — these are the textbook publishers' products. Because academic arenas are so controlled and the audience captive, this is where the money is in the world of publishing. And, because of this, the market is the hardest to break into.

Scholarly publishing, also known as academic publishing, is for such institutions as museums (Smithsonian and Metropolitan for example) and universities. Professors and teachers are re-quired to write books if they want to get tenure and they need someone to publish these books. Generally, the only folks who read these books are other academics.

Reference publishers are those who primarily print works of reference, often referred to as hard reference. Their main cus-tomers are libraries and librarians across the country. Any kind of dictionaries or encyclopedias would likely fall into this publish-ing category.

Finally, there is the Mass Market. These are typically paper-back books of smaller than average size. Normally, these books are found not in major bookstores, but in drugstores and super-markets. Their size runs roughly 4 inches by 6 inches and is very recognizable on the racks at the discount stores. Much of the time these publishers produce fiction that is reprinted from pre-viously produced books.

The Web

Searching the Internet for a particular publisher's website could yield helpful information. Sites belonging to smaller houses tend to be simpler with more information for those interested in buying their books rather than advice for writers. After all, selling books and making money is the reason the publishers are in business.

As maintaining and producing web pages gets cheaper, easier and more common, more houses are getting on the bandwagon and hosting a website. They're noticing it reduces phone calls when the information callers seek is posted on the site. Contact information including e-mail addresses, phone numbers, addresses, departments and (editorial) employee names are oftentimes easily accessible.

Online catalogs of past, present and future publications give an author a good feel for what the house typically produces and the flavor of what they might want in a book proposal. In addition, a history of the publishing company gives insight into who its employees are, how they are to work with and how long the company has been around. Chances are, if the website is well-organized and filled with helpful information, it's a reflection of how the company operates.

For those of you who are active on the Internet (and I imagine most of you are), there is a website for writers at www.writersmarket.com. This site sells itself by saying it's "your wired key to publishing success, providing the most comprehensive — and always up-to-date — market contact info available, with electronic tools you won't find anywhere else." The annual service fee is $29.99 with a 30-day money back guarantee. If you prefer a monthly plan, it's $2.99 and you can cancel anytime.

The offerings online from these sorts of services (and there are quite a few) are such things as:

• A Submission Tracker to help manage manuscripts, submissions and the status of queries and assignments

• Contact information for hundreds of literary agents and agencies

• Standard pay rates and submission guidelines

• Links to research resources and writing sites

Multiple Submissions

During your search for a publisher, you will often see the phrase "multiple submissions accepted." What does this mean? Well, the general rule among writers is that you should not submit an article or book proposal to multiple publishers or outlets at the same time. It's considered unprofessional to send out simultaneous submissions without approval.

The reason for this is to avoid the embarrassment of having multiple companies accept your idea and then you have to tell one of them you already sold your book to someone else. If this happens to you, there is a black mark against your name for the next time around.

There are differing opinions on this subject. Some writers think it's unfair to have to wait anywhere from one to six months to hear back from a publisher. And then, more than likely, the proposal is rejected. At this rate, it takes years to find a publisher to actually buy a book and then it still has to be written.

One option to circumvent this dilemma is to send out "multiple submissions" and be open and to be honest about it. If the information is disclosed, say on the cover page, then everyone knows up-front that any number of people could be looking at the idea. All you need to do is type the words multiple submission on the proposal. Everyone knows what you mean. This way, the first publisher to accept and buy your work is the one that gets you as their author.

Being open about the fact that you are sending simultaneous submissions may have negative repercussions on your success. When editors see the note declaring your submission practice, they may have mixed reactions. Sometimes it won't bother the editor at all, and may even push them to act more quickly if they like the proposal. Other editors may find it insulting and feel you have pitted them against others in the field — with a resulting rejection of your work.

An alternative is to limit the number of submissions you send out at one time. Say, for example, you send out only three and then wait to hear back from these publishers before sending out three more. Then, if your proposal is accepted by all three, you won't have quite as many to turn down.

Large Publishing Houses vs. Small Ones

Coming up with a book idea and putting together the proposal is essential to getting a book published. But who you send your book proposal to is just as crucial. As I mentioned earlier, large houses aren't interested in anything written for a narrow audience or anything highly specialized because it won't sell as well. They have large overhead and higher expenses, so they need to be able to make a sufficient amount of money to cover their costs and still make a profit. To you the writer, this means a tougher sell.

The larger publishing houses have more staff and more resources. This is a plus for you, as they have a budget for graphic artists, editors, proofreaders, typesetters and copyeditors. These people work closely with an author, and take some of the load off your shoulders. You write it, and they edit it, make it look pretty and very often have computer programs or designated personnel to do the dreaded index, annotations, footnotes and the table of contents.

In addition to these advantages, a large house may negotiate a better contract that pays more and offers higher royalties because they can afford to. And, they probably have more clout in the book world to get your work more exposure. Your book may sit on a more prominent bookshelf or table and be pushed harder by the sales people if there is a connection with an influential publisher.

Marketing and distribution are vital to the success of any publication. Each season, as the house unveils its list to the world, it markets them with vigor. But how much vigor depends on the size of that house and the available funds in the promotion budget.

According to the Book Industry Study Group, smaller publishing houses are doing a better job by far of marketing their titles than are the large companies. The larger publishing houses tend to stick with traditional methods of marketing by getting as many titles as possible into the biggest bookstores possible. Then they sit back and wait for the sales to happen. The smaller folks have fewer titles and therefore more time to push each one.

The big guys have a wide array of subjects covered on their

lists and are forced to market to a very broad and often not very unfamiliar market. The smaller houses carry more specialized lists and know their readers and the subject well. This, in the end, allows them to market more effectively.

Some say that how-to books, self-improvement books, travel books and the like sell themselves. The logic is that if someone makes the decision to improve their life, travel or learn something they browse the book section and buy the books without seeing any advertising or promotion.

The marketing bottom line, according to insiders, is based on the size of the publishing houses' budget. Larger houses have a larger budget for marketing, book tours, promotional materials and convention exhibits. A small publishing house has less capital available to fund these sorts of things for all their books and may be able to do so only for one title at a time.

It isn't uncommon for the larger houses to make an initial push with your book and then wait to see if the public rushes to buy it. If that doesn't happen or sales are average, they remainder (see Chapter 9's section called "Life Cycle,") the book after its first print run and then it goes out of print.

On the other hand, a smaller house keeps plugging away at the marketing of your book without giving up on it. In their view, the average sales add up over the long term. The more time the book is for sale, the more profit it can make for the house.

To the small guy, sales from the first run of books, pays for the costs of production, and any revenues from additional printings are mostly free and clear gain. With this formula the book can be a modest revenue generator for years and make small profits for the house and the author for a significant amount of time.

Logically, a smaller house has fewer expenses, such as payroll, office space rents and overhead. The bigger publishers they don't need as much money to operate and, hence, make a profit from books with lower sales numbers.

Have you ever read a bad book you couldn't finish? Most of us have. You probably asked yourself, "Why anyone would publish something so uninteresting?" Well, here's one reason: the big houses want to maintain the very valuable shelf space they are allotted at the bookstores. If they don't have books to pack those racks, they could lose the space for those times when they do have the books to fill them. Therefore, they publish inferior books they know aren't good, as fillers for the retail shelves and if they sell a few while they're at it, all the better.

Looking at regional publishers might be something you want to think about if you decide to try the smaller publishers instead of the big firms. In an effort to support the local economy and local "artists," a publisher in your area may be more willing to take a chance on someone who lives in that location. It might even save them a few bucks if they decide to do a local marketing campaign.

Another upside to using local or regional publishers is if the subject matter is somewhat regional. For example, if you want to write a book on *Antebellum Homes of the South*, and you live in the South, a regional publisher is going to be a good bet.

The Post Office

Once your proposal is complete and you have your list of potential publishers at hand, it's time to prepare the envelopes. It's best to use large, preferably manila, envelopes (quality envelopes with your logo make a great first impression). Never fold or squeeze your proposal into an envelope that is too small. If it doesn't fit, hoof it to the nearest office supply or stationary store and get some that are the right size. Don't scrimp, it looks unprofessional.

You will see the acronym SASE often in the publishing business. This stands for Self Addressed Stamped Envelope and it's required for you to send one along with your manuscript or proposal in order to get any kind of response from a publisher. If you do not include a SASE, your manuscript goes straight to the recycle bin.

Type four address labels, two with your name and address and two with the publisher's name and address. Place one label with your name and address in the top left-hand corner of one envelope and in the center of the other envelope. Place one label with the publisher's name and address in the top left-hand corner of one envelope and in the center of the other. Fold the envelope that is addressed to you and put it inside the other envelope along with your paper clipped proposal. Don't seal it yet.

Now you are off to the post office to get the envelopes weighed. Ask them to weigh the envelope and give you that amount of postage for each outgoing package. Then, take the return envelope out and have them weigh the proposal again. The postage amount should go down a little. Buy this amount of postage for each SASE and put it on the return envelopes. Then put the SASE's inside the outgoing mail and seal the envelope. Say a prayer over them for good luck and stuff them into the mailbox.

In order to avoid anyone stealing her idea and her work, one artist I know makes an extra copy of the work she is sending out, seals it, and mails herself a copy via registered mail. That way, if she sees her work appear somewhere it shouldn't, she can get her still-sealed, registered envelope and show it to a judge as proof the work is hers. It is her way of protecting herself.

Rejections

Your proposal may go through several hands for review before making it to someone who can say yes to buy it. Titles for those in these authoritative positions can read as acquisitions editor, commissioning editor, sponsoring editor, assistant acquisitions editor, editorial assistant or assistant editor.

The larger the publishing house, the more people get a chance to scrap or pass your idea onward and upward. But first, your proposal arrives and sits for a few months while piles of previous mail are handled. In publishing lingo, the name for the stack where unsolicited manuscripts and proposals sit is the **slush-pile**.

In older circles you may hear the term **unsol**, a short version of the word "unsolicited," which means the same as slush-pile. This word is not as commonly used but you may still hear it and it means the same thing — semi-abandoned envelopes.

Another interesting and historic term meaning unsolicited or slush-pile is over-the-transom. The fable goes that writers who were desperate for an editor or publisher to see their work tossed the manuscript through the transom (a smallish window that opened horizontally above the door to allow air flow), and hoped the person inside would be kind enough to take a look at the flying script.

The first person to see the book proposal is likely to be the person who opens the mail. If he sees there is no SASE or it is single spaced copy, chances are he'll toss the package into the trash. If it passes muster here, however, it may go to a junior editor. If he likes what he sees, he'll pass the information on to at least one or two more editors. Finally your proposal may make it to a senior editor or publisher who determines if the idea goes to the acquisition board.

In a smaller house, one person may make all these decisions. This, of course, makes selling an idea easier because as a rule if you get two or more people in one room discussing anything there will be many differing opinions, likes and dislikes.

Let's assume the proposal makes it to the acceptance stage. You then get a letter, e-mail or phone call telling you the publishing house wants to work with you on your proposed project. That is the best feeling in the world and your chest swells with pride. Now it's time for you to agree and negotiate the contract.

If, however, the publisher doesn't accept your proposal, you get a rejection letter along with your SASE. It's the most depressing feeling and a great blow to your ego, but don't get too down. Instead pick up the pieces and send the proposal out again.

The rejection can come in any of several forms. Sometimes, in the worst case scenario, you never hear anything at all back from the publisher. The only way to know for sure what happened is to write again or call. This can be frustrating, as they probably won't even remember your package.

Others send out a generic little postcard with an "x" next to the reason for the rejection. The potential checklist might include:

• We are not currently publishing works in this category

• We have on our list already, or are planning to publish in the near future, a similar book

• The market for your book seems too specialized for our list, which is of a more general nature

• The budget for the current publishing year has been committed for the season and we are not allocating any funds for new books until the end of next year.

SAGE ADVICE

Some tell you that they liked your idea but they have a full publishing roster for the next year and could you please send your proposal back in the six months for their next buying cycle.

Still others say they liked your proposal and you did a great job, but unfortunately your idea doesn't fit in with their immediate plans. They may say they will keep your well-written proposal on file for future reference and possibly use it as a source when looking for a potential author.

The bottom line is: they don't want to publish your book, and that hurts.

A handwritten note on your cover letter returned to you from a kindly editor makes the rejection blow less severe. Many in the industry go this route while wishing you the best of luck in finding a place for your manuscript. If you get a penned note from the editor, take it as a compliment, and assume they at least respect the effort you put into the work.

If the note expresses a reason for the rejection and it's something you can fix, then do so before you send it out to the next house. For example, if the editor writes that he liked the general story line but found the Old English too difficult to read, modernize it and send it out again.

Rejection letters sometimes arrive due to poor timing on your part. If you're proposing a Christmas book, be sure to send the proposal early enough in the year to allow delivery of your book at Christmastime. Don't send the idea in November for that Christmas, because it's too late.

Don't be too dejected when you get a rejection letter — everyone has and everyone will continue to do so. It's the industry's way of coping with the enormous number of proposals received. It doesn't necessarily mean you are stupid or that you can't write. Pearl S. Buck, for example, received a rejection letter at the same time she was notified of winning the Nobel Prize for Literature! Whatever you do, don't give up.

9. WHAT YOU NEED AND WANT

Essentials

Without a doubt, you must have a writing spot to call your own. This is a place where your research papers won't be disturbed and your pens won't disappear. It's somewhere you can leave everything as it is, come back tomorrow and pick right up where you left off.

Your sanctuary doesn't have to be fancy. There's no need for leather panels and a secretary. A simple table and comfortable chair in a removed part of the house or room will suffice. It makes you feel like a professional writer. Without this place you won't focus properly on the task at hand and the outcome suffers.

Speaking of time, this is as critical as a personal writing space. Set a schedule for yourself and stick to it no matter what. There are so many distractions − kids, television, dinner, fun − and this is particularly true if you have a regular job and are trying to write a book proposal in your spare time. The only way you'll achieve success is to draft a writing schedule (pin it in a prominent place). To be effective, you must try not to deviate from this appointed writing time, but don't punish yourself if you do. Just do better next time.

Possibly, the most critical tool to achieve success is a viable computer. That's not to say there aren't writers today who succeeded using a manual typewriter, but life is much simpler working with a computer and a good printer. Doing research on the Internet and communications via e-mail won't hurt progress either.

Such things as a stapler, paper clips, scissors, pens, paper, printer ink, stamps, and other office supplies are essential to your peace of mind. You can't keep running to the store or to another room to scrounge for these things when you need them. Keeping these items handy allows you to stay focused, work the scheduled time and get the job done.

In order to present a professional looking product, your pages need a header and page numbers. All word processing programs have tools for inserting text at the top of a page (in the 1-inch top margin) that runs consecutively from page to page. The text is in a box of its own and looks almost transparent or translucent in your document.

It's customary to put the author's last name, a dash, and the book title aligned to the left side of the header. Then, in the center of the top of the page inside the header insert a page number or folio.

With this identifying information, all the editor has to do is glance at the top of the page to know which manuscript he is reading or which page he was last looking at. In the event the pages get dropped or disorganized, it's an easy task to re-assemble them.

Some writers like to use the footer, or the bottom 1-inch margin of each page to put the folio or some of the proposal's information. I feel, however, that keeping it all in one place at the top makes it easier to find and easier to read. Sometimes, publishers have a specific style they want their authors to follow when it comes to the header presentation. If so, do it their way.

The nice thing about headers and footers is that they take care of themselves. If you add or subtract fifty pages or fifty sentences everywhere or anywhere in your proposal, these nifty header lines simply add or subtract themselves to and from the copy.

If your title is too long to fit at the top with the centered folio, it's acceptable either to put the page number on the right side of the page, on the second line down, or center it in the footer. For example, the top of my pages for this book's proposal looked something like this:

Vachon - Getting Your Book Published   **32**

WHAT YOU NEED AND WANT

When you sign a contract you'll notice the publisher expects you to turn in one (sometimes two) printed copies of the finished manuscript. The accepted paper size is 8-1/2 inches by 11 inches printed on one side only. Don't try to scrimp. If you do, the publisher pays someone else to do it and charges you, or asks you to print the entire thing again. I know it seems like a waste of paper, but it's the industry norm and not worth balking at.

You'll need to submit an electronic version too. This means on a computer diskette or CD in a format. The publishing industry for the most part uses Macs, but publishers can convert most documents from a PC. Let them know what software and format you use.

A word of caution here, please, please save several copies of the proposal or manuscript somewhere other than your hard drive. When I wrote my first book, my computer crashed and I only had the original copy I was working on. I was in tears! I took my hard drive to a systems recovery specialist and he recovered all but one or two chapters. The stress was tremendous, it was expensive and I lost valuable time.

Now I have the copy on my hard drive, a copy on my laptop and a copy on a disk. I keep them all updated at all times and the disk copy is in a safe place. Now, of course, I'll never have computer problems again — yeah right!

Standard Editing Symbols

Editors and others in the field use the symbols on the next page to indicate text changes. The marks are universally understood among writers, editors, proofreaders, text processors, publishers and printers.

A professional proofreader puts a mark (usually a line or caret) where the change goes and writes the correction in the margin. An editor makes corrections within the line rather than in the margin (in part because an editor's changes are typically more extensive), which is why editors prefer, actually insist, on working with double-spaced copy.

PROOFREADING MARKS

Proofing Mark		Example	After Change
/	lowercase	Ǧreat force	great force
≡	capitalize	the simplest	The simplest
‾	italics	sweet offerings	*sweet offerings*
∿	bold	tremendous show	**tremendous show**
∿	bold italics	I'm published!	***I'm published!***
⊙	add period	then sleeping ⊙	then sleeping.
∧	insert (comma)	green‚red and blue	green, red and blue
∧	(space)	gravy‸train	gravy train
⌣	close space	riding the tid e⌣	riding the tide
℮	delete	he went went℮	he went
¶	start paragraph	¶ On the second day...	
∿	transpose	rivre	river

Writer's Guidelines

Most publishers have standard writer's guidelines for authors. If you have any doubts about who the publisher is and what sort of manuscripts they are looking for, look them up, call them and ask them to send you their writer's guidelines. They will.

Sometimes they may ask you to send a SASE in a letter requesting the guidelines and then they'll send them to you. Sometimes they tell you they are not accepting any new unsolicited manuscripts or proposals at this time.

Once you get the guidelines and read them, there will be no doubt as to whether you're sending your book to the right place or not. They clearly say what the publisher wants, when and from whom.

As I mentioned earlier in this book, there are many reference guides available at the library that list needs and addresses of publishers. This may make it redundant to solicit writer's guidelines and be less time consuming. However, they may be outdated.

If publishers have a website, they may have their submission specifications available to download as a PDF. This saves them from having to answer phone calls from authors asking for writer's guidelines. And, the publisher is able to keep the guidelines up to date.

Don't Look Like a Beginner

Publishers and editors can spot a rookie from a mile away. There are some basic cardinal sins writers should avoid. Dodge the most common and obvious errors by following these tips.

When you set up your manuscript or proposal on your computer, learn very quickly how to make the text double-spaced. Editors and proofreaders need this extra space to keep their sanity! Can you imagine reading and editing single spaced text all day? Their eyes would fall out.

Besides, in order to do their jobs and mark up the copy, they need the extra room to write in. That way the typesetter or person entering the changes to the manuscript can read and follow the marks/directions.

Show passion. If you are bored and drone on about whatever it is you write, just think how bored the editor or publisher is. Without passion, you don't stand a chance. If there is no passion, you need to rethink and reconsider your subject matter.

Just imagine someone telling a story. If they use a monotone and no emphasis in their voice, it's hard to stay engrossed no matter how great the story is. The same is true of a book proposal. If you show enthusiasm, it indicates to the editor you know your subject, feel strongly about it and can probably write a captivating book.

Spelling is critical to the success of your book proposal. If the copy you send in is full of errors and spelling mistakes, it's natural that the publisher assumes this is the standard for all your work. They won't want to have any part of working with you on a manuscript, much less publish your book. I'd suggest you use a good dictionary and learn to check spelling on your computer. Use both sources for help, as most computers' spelling software isn't exact.

If I had to pick the number one pet peeve of editors, I would say it's spelling their names incorrectly. Let's say you spent months coming up with your book idea, writing an organized proposal, carefully selecting the correct publishing venue, finding out the right contact's name and address and then you spell that name wrong. It looks really unprofessional, makes people mad, and tips the scales out of your favor. Try hard not to do this.

Staples are a marvelous invention when used to keep the appropriate documents together. A book proposal or manuscript is not that document. Please don't use staples, or you will have annoyed publishers and editors saying bad words as they work on your proposal (that is, if the staples don't stop them from working on your proposal altogether).

For anything you need to pin together, use paper clips. They are a marvelous invention too. If the paper clip is too small, use a binder clip or a rubber band if you must.

There are two common dashes used in writing. One is called an en dash (–) and the other an em dash (—). If you want to use a hyphen-like dash in your text to separate copy, use an em dash. Most novices use two hyphens (-) typed next to each other. The em dash is what publishers use. This may seem trivial to you, and it probably is, but if you get it right, the editor/publisher might be impressed.

On occasion, the publisher specifies what style they want you to follow. This is especially true if you are writing a particular genre or a series written by several authors. They want all their books to look identifiably the same in an effort to get satisfied customers to buy their other books and to establish a brand.

The publisher dictates typeface, point size, heading size, sub-heading size and indentation/tab specifics. It gets rather complicated, but try to follow the guidelines closely if you do get these instructions. Most publishers have a typesetter go over these styles before the book goes to print, but the more you help out, the more likely another book contract has your name on it. It's always best not to get labeled as a temperamental writer, even if some of us are.

If the styles and formats aren't specified, make up a simple format of your own and be as consistent as you can with it. For example, indent your paragraphs consistently; make all main headings bold with only the first letters capitalized (easier to read) and centered with 14 point type; make sub-heads lower case with an initial letter capitalized, bold and flush left.

If you are a published author, let's say someone like Pat Conroy or John Grisham, you certainly don't need to worry about such trivia. The many editors and proofreaders on staff take care of their errors. But if you are a first-time writer, these details make a difference in a clean and professional presentation. This is particularly true with smaller publishers who have smaller staffs and don't feel the need to (and can't) pamper you until you become a best selling author.

Contract Negotiations

When negotiating the contract for your first book, you probably are given a take-it or leave-it offer. Take it! Large publishers receive hundreds of manuscripts each day, so if you get this far, jump on the chance to get published.

The good news is that in the United States alone, there are 80,000 new books published each year. Your book idea has as good a chance as anyone else's if you present it properly.

A lot depends on whether you are using an agent or not, but don't be afraid to ask questions if you don't have one. Don't hesitate to let them know you are doing this for the first time and ask the editor or publisher to guide you through it. Find out exactly what is expected of you. If they are worth their salt, they answer your questions fully and respect you for having the courage to approach them. Use your common sense to decide if you are being treated fairly.

The most essential details a contract includes are when the manuscript is due, how long it should be, the royalties and the advance if any. After checking and approving these facts, which really should have been agreed to some time ago, take the time to read the rest of the contract. This helps avoid and nasty surprises later on.

Be sure you are able to deliver the entire manuscript by the due date. Nothing frustrates an editor more than having to chase a writer down for work owed. It's unfortunate that writers have a reputation for being temperamental and tardy. A publisher told me once that I was the first writer ever to turn a manuscript in on time without being nagged — I was amazed.

From the other side of the desk, with my editor's hat on, I can confirm that writers are often behind when turning in their copy. It's amazing how many weird and original excuses people give for late work. The best one was when the writer's grandmother died for the fifth time! The most original, "I dropped the manuscript pages onto the train track and the engineer wouldn't let me go down and get them." The publisher doesn't want to hear excuses.

When it comes to length, verify that not only the number printed pages are specified, but also the word count. The size of the book, the number of words per page, the type size and line spacing can change the number of final pages drastically. Be clear about this to avoid having to write or cut thousands of words at the last minute.

When it comes to getting paid for photos, graphics and charts make sure you bring it up. Sometimes it's standard in a contract but sometimes it's not. If you are providing the images (especially for the book cover) make sure you ask to get paid over and above the advance. Typically, with a smaller publishing house, the fee is smaller — anywhere from $150.00 to $300.00 for inside photos and $500.00 to $1,000 for a cover or back cover. This varies widely.

Once your successful book sells the first print run of 5,000 copies, the publisher will likely ask you to do a revised and updated second edition. Once again, they take a look at the market potential and may even ask you to do a new "mini-proposal." Some books seem to go on indefinitely and become household standards with multiple editions.

When you get to the point of doing a second edition, you can expect to sign another contract much the same as the first one. You will also most likely be offered the same payment terms. If you feel comfortable doing so now that you proved yourself, you may want to discuss the possibility of an increase either in the advance amount or in the royalty percentage. If you don't ask, they aren't going to offer.

WHAT YOU NEED AND WANT

The amount of editing and re-writing is something you should consider discussing during your contract negotiations. If it's a smaller house, your work won't be as heavily edited or changed by as many staff members. With a larger publisher, the changes may be significant and your voice may get lost. If you feel strongly about this, it may be possible to ask that you see and have input for all changes made. This however, is a privilege usually reserved for the most successful authors.

Before you can negotiate a contract, you must decide what you want. If getting published is your first priority, take the contract and don't try to finagle a better deal. Once you have established yourself as a regular with that publishing house or you have written several books, then you may have leverage for negotiation on the next contract.

If money is your main concern, then you'll have a much harder time the first time around and may have to consider giving up. Review your proposal and estimate how much time and research go into the writing of your book. Once you've figured out the number of hours you think it takes to get the book done, divide the advance offer into the hours and see how much you'll be making per hour. Then assume you'll sell all the first print run books and add that royalty to the total. Is it worth it? Only you can say.

Perhaps there's room somewhere in the middle for you to negotiate. Be prepared when you call the editor or publisher and have your facts at-the-ready. You might say for example, that the research involved for this book is extensive compared to other books of its type because... Or, the length of the book in your proposal was considerably shorter than the length the publisher wants. So is there any way he could possibly find a few extra dollars to bump up the fee and make the deal work?

With a careful, creative and diplomatic approach, you might find the editor is willing to take money from the art budget or the marketing budget and toss some your way.

An exchange is another possibility. For example, you might say you can produce the charts and illustrations yourself and save the house from hiring a freelancer. In exchange for the work you can collect the fee the artist would have received.

Some contracts are one or two pages long and written in plain

English that anyone can understand. These types of contracts cover the basics and not much more. They are easy to follow but may leave out decisions on issues that come up later.

Other contracts are so complicated you literally need an attorney or an agent who specifically works in the publishing industry to review it. It may be possible to hire one of these professionals for a one-time fee. If there is a great deal of money riding on the deal, it may be worth your while. Otherwise you'll have to read and understand it yourself or trust the publisher to be fair.

Advances

It's typical to be offered a sum of money for the work in question. This is called an advance. The advance amount, if there is one, varies widely. It can be anywhere from $1,000 to millions. But, for a new author, the amount is likely to be on the lower end of the scale unless there is a great agent involved and, even then, there's no guarantee.

A lot depends on the size of the house, the type of book, hardcover or paperback, whether this is your first book and your negotiation skills. If you can charm the editor or publisher into paying you more that's great.

Many publishing houses aren't offering any advances. They feel the publishing industry has been hit hard and the author should share in the risks by getting paid only on actual sales not on potential sales.

The payment times vary with publishing houses. Generally, authors get half of the advance when the contract is signed and half when the manuscript is delivered. It may also stipulate in your contract that the manuscript must be approved before a check for the remaining portion of the advance is mailed.

If you are lucky enough to be offered an advance, think of it as a non-refundable loan against the future earnings of the book. The only way out for a publisher is if you fail to fulfill any or all parts of the contract.

The advance is subtracted from the royalties due you until enough books sell to cover it. Then you begin getting a check for royalties on books sold over and above the advance.

It's rare for a publisher to ask for his money back, but if you've turned out to be a poor investment for any reason other than poor sales numbers, it might happen. Don't give the publisher the opportunity to say the book did badly because it was late or wasn't factual. Write an exemplary book, with the right number of pages and deliver it on time.

If for some reason the book does not sell as the publisher anticipated, you won't be asked to give the money back. The house continues to try and market the book but eventually writes off the loss.

Royalties

The contract usually states that the publisher pays the author anywhere from five percent to twelve percent of the book price when it's sold. This is called a royalty.

There are many different ways a publishing house can define how they want to pay out their royalties to the authors and it may vary from book to book and writer to writer. But there are two ways most commonly stipulated in an author's contract. The first is list royalty the second is net royalty.

With net royalty, the contract may exclude the term "net" and simply say the royalty is calculated on the total retail price paid for the book. In other words, with net royalties, the author receives a percentage of the actual sales price. This is perhaps the most common payment method stipulated in author's contracts.

If the book is on sale or discounted in any way, the author receives the agreed upon percentage on that amount collected at the cash register, not on the actual price printed on the cover of the book. Say for example, the book's price upon publication is $18.95 but it is sold at the bookstore for $5.95, the writer's royalty is x percent of $5.95.

List royalty, on the other hand, states that no matter what amount is actually paid for the book, the author receives x percent of the price printed on the cover of the book. A book on sale or deeply discounted won't affect the royalty amount the author collects. If the book price was determined at the outset to be $18.95 but it sold at the bookseller for $5.95, the writer still collects x percent of $18.95 for each book bought. Naturally, this is a much better deal for the author and you can see why not many publishers choose this option.

Check your contract to see if the small print states your royalties are paid minus any returns. What the publisher is telling you is that if someone buys your book you'll get the royalty percentage agreed upon unless the customer returns that book to the bookseller. In effect, he is saying that book was never actually sold since the reader came back for his money and therefore you won't get paid your royalty for that returned book.

It seems the publishers are at the mercy of the book outlets. When it comes to returns the bookseller can return the unsold books for full and complete credit. If the book happens to be a paperback, the bookseller can send back only the ripped-off cover or a piece of the cover to satisfy the "return" qualification and get his full credit.

List or net royalties also apply to books sold overseas. Usually due to higher shipping, storage and distribution costs of doing business outside the US, the royalty percent is half the amount of sales inside the US. For example, if your contract is for 6 percent net royalty of all books sold in the US, then you'll collect a 3 percent royalty for all books sold overseas. If you anticipate your international sales are higher than your American sales, it may be worth negotiating an increase in the royalty percentage for overseas books sold.

It's typical for many publishers to vary the royalty percentage depending on the quantity of books sold. For example on a trade paperback the first 100,000 copies may garner the author six percent. On the next 25,000 books sold, the author receives seven percent. On any book quantities sold over 500,000, the author gets eight percent. Most of us won't be so lucky or get close to selling this many books but it isn't uncommon for the terms to be stipulated nonetheless. The publishers can afford to do this because the more books they sell the cheaper the cost to produce them. The initial expenses to print the book are the highest.

You should receive a royalty statement from the publisher at least every six months. It shows the total books sold (domestic and international), less returns. In most cases this is twice a year but sometimes quarterly depending on the bookkeeping method the publisher uses.

WHAT YOU NEED AND WANT

As books sell, the publisher adds up the royalties due you and deducts the advance from that amount until the books make enough to cover it. After it is all accounted for, you'll get royalty checks resulting from subsequent sales.

The publisher is required to keep track of all books sold, given away, damaged and unsalable. He is responsible for keeping up with your book from inception to demise. But the statements often don't say how many books were printed and how many are still available. Ask about this, as it helps tremendously in the tracking of your books if you have these numbers on each statement.

In general, you must trust the house to be honest and fair. The industry as a whole has a rocky reputation when it comes to accuracy (intentional or otherwise) of royalty statements, so it's worth paying attention to the details.

Keep track of your own statements as they arrive and ask the person who does the books or his assistant for help and an explanation if you get too confused. If you are certain there is a discrepancy you may want to consider an audit. For a fee you can hire a specialist for this industry who conducts the audit but you probably won't be popular with the house if you do so. To find such a person check with the National Writers Union or The Authors Guild.

Sample Royalty Statement

List Price: $18.95   **Total Books Sold Less Returns:** 1192
Books Sold in US: 1128   **Books Sold Overseas:** 64
Total USD Sales: $21,375.60 **Total Int'l. Sales:** $1,212.80
US Royalties: $1,282.54   **Int'l. Royalties:** $36.38
          (6%)   (3%)

Total Royalties This Half of 2002: $1,318.92
Advances Paid: $4,000
Books Sold to Date: 3414
Royalties Earned to Date: $3,762.33

Amount Due: $00.00

Copyrights

The argument of whether the work should be copyrighted in the name of the author or the publisher is one that never seems to go away. The details, laws and ramifications fill entire books and keep many lawyers busy for a lifetime.

The only time I feel this issue should be challenged is if the work in question will, without a doubt, generate millions of dollars for the copyright holder. Besides that, it isn't clear why this struggle takes place other than to satisfy a control issue.

If you have an agent, he will negotiate to have the work in your name. If this is your first book and the contract states the copyright belongs to the publisher, it probably isn't worth the fight especially as you aren't likely to win. It may even cost you the contract.

In general, non-fiction is copyrighted in the name of the publisher and fiction is copyrighted in the name of the author. Just as, in general, a writer has an agent if she writes fiction but doesn't have one if she writes non-fiction. In the final analysis, it may not be important in whose name the book is copyrighted. What may be important is who controls what rights (and there are many) while the book is in print.

For example, you may have a publishing contact in Africa who wants to translate the book into Swahili and distribute it there. Should you be able to do this on your own or should the publisher control the negotiations and get a cut? If the editor is going to have the publishing house's translation department translate the book into five other languages, then it probably should be their right, not yours. But it's your contact that wants to do the translating into Swahili. See what I mean when I say it can be complicated?

The all-rights contract states that the publisher has the right to all possible sources of income for the book including reprints both nationally and internationally. Some authors make a great deal of money from reprinting portions of their books. One writer I know says he makes ten percent of his income from reprints. That's nothing to sneeze at.

Negotiating this part of your contract, if you think you can reprint all or part of the book and make money, may be worth your while. If, however, you are intimidated because you never found a market for reprints of your other work, leave it up to the publisher, but make sure you're in for a cut of the proceeds. This seems only fair.

In order for there to be a book, you must transfer the rights for that book to the publisher. If this doesn't happen, there can't be a book with that publishing house. By agreeing to the transfer of rights, you are giving the publisher permission to publish your work. This is a separate issue from who gets the copyright, which often confuses first-time writers.

Your publisher automatically registers your work with the copyright office as a matter of course. He may do it in your name or in his, but it must done to protect the house and/or you in case of a legal battle.

If the work were not filed with the copyright office anyone could reproduce it or parts of it and use it in without permission. If it becomes necessary to stop someone from using the work without authorization, the copyright is the legal method of doing so from the court's perspective.

If your book becomes unavailable because it has sold out or is no longer being printed, the rights in most cases automatically revert back to the author. Obviously, a publisher who doesn't plan to re-print the book won't want to keep the rights to it. They don't really care what happens to it at this point and are happy for you to have the rights back.

To say more than the very basics here would take too long and is not the point of the book. Suffice it to say, the publisher does this all day long and you certainly should understand and know what you are getting into, but let him do what he does best and has done with many authors before you.

If you feel really strongly about something in the contract, talk to a copyright lawyer (literary property lawyer) or look in your local library for more detailed books on the subject.

The Publisher's Responsibilities

Many people, when writing their first book are afraid to ask the publisher what their role is in the process and some publishers like it that way. My advice is that you clarify anything you don't understand before getting into trouble by committing to something that's not what you thought it was.

The publisher is bound to know that you haven't done this before and more than likely wants things to be clear for both your sakes. He doesn't want to be surprised any more than you do, so don't hesitate to ask.

If asking what you perceive to be stupid questions scares the heck out of you, then take a trip to the library, the Internet or a bookstore and read everything they have on publishing. This will answer most your inquiries that aren't answered here and you will be a better-informed author ready to tackle whatever comes your way.

There are some less than honest or, "ethically-challenged" publishers out there, but, for the most part, I think you'll that find they fulfill their end of the publishing bargain. Of course they have a vested interest in doing the job right because it produces better books and more sales.

In traditional publishing, once an author prepares a book proposal or query letter, and the publisher accepts it, that author is contracted by that publisher to write the book. At that point the publisher agrees to incur all costs associated with producing, marketing, selling and distributing said book.

To make a contract more appealing, some publishers have a way of offering an author some perks that don't actually cost them any cash, but they aren't required to do so. For example, if you don't have an office or a place to write, the publishing house might be willing to let you use an empty office and perhaps throw in office supplies and equipment including a phone, computer, printer and copier. This saves you overhead expenses but doesn't affect the publisher's bottom line too much.

If your book requires a great deal of research and associated expenses such as travel, postage and interviews, an author can ask and sometimes get an allowance. This allowance would be paid up front and be over and above the advance amount. The proceeds would not have to be earned out against the royalties, as is the case with the advance.

Besides printing and distribution, publishers should agree at the beginning of the process to proofread and edit the book.

150

WHAT YOU NEED AND WANT

Depending on the size of the publishing house the extent of the editing can be very thorough or minimal. But, at the very least, it's the publisher's responsibility to check for spelling errors, typos and obvious grammatical mistakes the author missed (we of course hope there aren't any, but once in a while one or two slip by). There is nothing more embarrassing than having readers find these in the final product and tell you about them.

A publishing house with any kind of standards ensures that a consistent and attractive style flows throughout the book. The production or art department selects a typeface, size, and specifics for the text, headings, subheadings and any designs for the layout of the pages. In other words, the publishing house is responsible for a uniform overall look.

The publisher takes the initiative to get the book through the production phases of its life. It's his responsibility to make sure the book moves on schedule. This can take anywhere from six months to a year to cover each step of the process.

Initially, the manuscript is typeset, tracked and routed through the editing, proofreading and fact-checking departments. The galleys (or final output) are tracked by the publisher and given back to the author (if these are the author's contracted responsibilities) for such things as indexing, final proofing, cross-referencing and completion of the TOC.

In the meantime, the publisher is purchasing services and materials from printers and paper suppliers. Once the manuscript arrives at the printer, the publisher coordinates the completion of binding with the distributor.

The publishing house staff is supposed to make sure the books arrive at their destination in the correct quantities and at the correct time. It is all a fine-tuned and carefully choreographed dance with amazing results.

Warehousing and storing their books is an important obligation for the publisher. Because a book can be warehoused for years it's another expense a publisher takes into account when calculating production costs and profitability.

The books must be in a dry environment to avoid weathering, tearing or yellowing. The location must be bug-free to keep them from being eaten or used as nesting material. And, they must be carefully maintained and readily accessible at a moment's notice to be shipped off to bookstores around the country or the world.

A publisher is expected to sell the books he contracts authors to write. The selling of such books takes several forms, but the plan depends on how valuable he thinks your book is and how much money he has to spend on it. It may consist of distribution only or go the full gamut and include all kinds of promotional plans too.

Advertising in magazines, trade journals, newspapers and any other print, television or radio media is one rather expensive option. Many publishers don't go this route because they don't think a book will make enough money to cover these expenses and still make a profit.

A publicity campaign might be planned — with coverage in these same media venues — and may involve the appearance of the author at book signings or on television. All these details are in your contract. Again, this type of publicity is generally reserved for the books a publisher thinks will make a high return on the investment.

At the basic level, a publisher tries to sell the book to libraries, distributors, booksellers and/or stores. The distribution of a book is perhaps the most critical part of the team effort required for a successful publication.

Many of the publishing houses can't afford to maintain a sales force. Therefore, they depend on outside sources to meet their sales requirements. These people generally fall into three categories: those who sell books for multiple publishing houses, independent distributors who sell books for a living and travel all over the country or the world, and wholesalers who receive orders for books and fill those orders. It's up to the publisher to decide which is the most effective distribution/sales resource in terms of cost effectiveness and sales ratios.

Publishers offer to give the author a certain number of free copies when the book comes off the press. The amount varies, but somewhere between two and seven is the norm. A deciding factor is if the book is hardcover or paperback. Because hardback is more expensive to produce, there may be fewer of them.

This is a good place for the pro-agent argument, as an agent is likely to get the publisher to accept responsibility for more than a novice writer will, simply because she knows what to ask for and how to trade for it. What I'm saying is, the publisher is accountable for the basics (editing, printing, designing, marketing and distributing) but may be talked into doing more by an agent (or writer) with good bargaining skills.

Vanity Publishers

Vanity or subsidy publishers are everywhere, and they're quite simply not responsible for much of anything when you read the fine print of your contract. I think I can safely say you can count on a bitter taste in your mouth if you decide to work with one of these companies.

To find a vanity publisher, look in the back of magazines and in free flyers attached to junk mail. Ads that say things like, "Are you a book author in need of a publisher?" or "Let us publish your book," will clue you in as to who they are.

The advertisements from vanity publishers sound great. On the surface it looks like you share the costs of publishing and marketing your book with a company that really cares. The truth of the matter is that you'll incur costs up front for marketing and production, and they can end up owning your book.

In many instances, vanity publishers won't follow through with the selling or marketing of the book. They'll slither out of harm's way by doing a bare minimum to technically satisfy the contract. In a court of law, they did what they said they would do — but just barely, and you won't have any recourse but to walk away having learned a hard lesson.

After spending the money to get your book published with a vanity publisher, you may not want to commit more financial resources to pay a lawyer. At least this is what the vanity publisher hopes.

If you get a call from a publisher who loved your proposal and must publish your book but asks you to contribute money in order to do so — *run far and run fast.* He is probably a vanity publisher. The only exception to this rule would be if you are dealing with a reputable university press where it's commonly accepted for authors to give the press a subvention (money up front) to defray publishing costs.

Using reputable sources to find the names and addresses of legitimate publishing houses and presses steers you clear of this situation. The most popular and reliable source is the *Association of American University Presses Directory* (AAUP Directory) available at your local library.

Contact from an effusive (that right there should raise your "beware" antenna!) editor sends you into an orbit of happiness, and it is difficult to think clearly and consider whether he is in fact a vanity publisher. If you get caught up in the moment, try not to commit to anything until you check with writers/publishers organizations and associations to confirm his authenticity.

Legitimate industry publishers, reviewers and booksellers seldom, if ever, deal with these subsidy companies. In fact, they shun them. Any marketing efforts you attempt through traditional and reputable means after publishing your book with a vanity publisher will likely fall on deaf ears. Your book either gathers dust in your basement or is branded forever as a second-class citizen.

These folks have a bad reputation — deservedly so, in my opinion. However, for the sake of fairness I should say that, if you simply must get your book published and are willing to pay to have it done, a subsidy or vanity publisher takes all the necessary steps and delivers a book (of perhaps questionable quality) to your door.

Think long and hard before going this route.

Life Cycle

The life cycle of a book varies widely. Sometimes, the publishers decide to put a book out of its misery after the first print run because of poor sales numbers. Or perhaps the book was very time specific and is now out of date thereby putting itself out of print.

For smaller publishing houses, it's possible to stretch the availability and therefore sales of a book out for years if there are no overwhelming marketing costs associated with it. The bigger publishers have a much more restrictive time frame for selling their books and may be forced to remainder (publishing lingo for "retired") titles after an average selling season.

It's the publisher's obligation to let the author know when his book is about to be remaindered. At this point, the author is given the chance to buy as many books as he wants. Whether the author decides to sell them on his own or have a bonfire with them — it's usually fine with the publishing house.

So much of the success of a book depends on how well and where it's marketed. Barnes and Noble Booksellers, B.Dalton and Borders are great places to sell your book, but that doesn't mean you can't make money from books sold at discount stores, outlets and to special interest audiences.

It's not uncommon to hear about an author who bought all her books from the publisher as they were about to be remaindered and then turned around and sold them all herself through book clubs and catalogs.

If the book is not a best-seller anymore, but is still worth reading, the publisher may decide to auction it off to the highest bidder. In this scenario, the book most likely ends up in the hands of a discount bookseller or remainder dealer and goes on to grace night stands for a few more years.

Dealers often buy what stock is left of a particular title. The prices they offer (and usually get) for these titles are well below what it took to produce the book in the first place. In fact they pay only pennies on each dollar of the cover price. A publisher won't make any profit from selling to remainders dealers but gets a quick inflow of cash that he wouldn't have collected otherwise, and gains valuable warehouse space.

There are even cases where the books in stock and the reprint rights were sold to another publisher who successfully brought them back into circulation. The books become profitable again largely due to renewed marketing efforts and a fresh perspective.

A book about to be retired — if not sold to a discount distributor — is sent off to the giant recycling bin for shredding, only to be revived and used in another form. Perhaps it comes back as printing paper for the next project to come off the presses.

A good book that sells consistently and whose information

continues to be helpful to readers can go on generating modest royalties for the author long after the writer is too old to type.

Final Word

Thank you for taking the time to read this book, I'm appreciative. I wish you the very best of luck with the hard work and deliberate planning ahead. As the saying goes, success is one percent inspiration and 99 percent perspiration.

If you have the drive to write and create that means you are an artist and it would be a transgression to waste that passion. Even if you don't become a millionaire from your prose, the gratification you'll feel as you shape and complete your creation will thrill you beyond words.

I sincerely hope these pages helped you overcome any trepidation you felt by disclosing all the secrets of getting your book published. The rest is up to you. Good luck!

Notes

Notes

Notes